ENDOR‹

Dr. Larry Ollison's new book *Hidden Mysteries and the Bible* equips the saints with vital information that is mostly avoided by pastors today. Ollison peels back the layers of deception that has been meticulously and surreptitiously orchestrated by the Dragon, i.e., Satan. Ollison draws his information from a trusted source—our Bibles. So dive in and prepare to be armed with the truth that will help all of us get through these turbulent and unprecedented times.

Bravo!

Dr. L. A. Marzulli
CEO, Spiral of Life

Hidden Mysteries and the Bible is a fascinating read. You will have trouble putting it down as I did. I have always enjoyed asking the strange and inscrutable questions—the ones that required more than just a perfunctory response by those in authority. These types of questions and topics are exactly what Dr. Larry Ollison brings forth in this book and he does not shy away from giving in-depth answers. In addition, it was a joy to learn more about Dr. Ollison as he shares tidbits from his own life and spiritual journey in seeking to gain a deeper understanding of God's universe and the mysteries of the Bible.

Will you agree with everything in the book? You absolutely do not need to in order to gain a greater understanding of these complex topics. I really appreciate the way in which Dr. Ollison makes sure the reader understands that there are different points of view on many of these topics and they do not affect anyone's salvation. Yet you will absolutely enjoy the journey in discussing topics like this that are rarely found together in any one book. You will be blessed, encouraged, and stimulated to greater thinking!

Mondo Gonzales
Media Host, Author
Co-host at Prophecy Watchers

First, let me compare Dr. Ollison's *Hidden Mysteries and the Bible* to my favorite meal: pizza super supreme! A collection of various ingredients assembled into a delicious undertaking. Starting with 16 hot topics, each divided into numerous related parts, the reader takes a journey through the supernatural elements of the Bible, Christianity, eschatology, and the secular world.

Mixed with some astounding personal experiences, biblical facts, satanic/demonic attempts at deception, and worldwide anxiety over a sense that something ominous is in the air, we then see why all the ingredients result in the final product—an alert from Dr. Ollison: "There is a cosmic war that has been raging from the beginning of time. This war is between good and evil, but deeper than that, the war is actually between the Creator and His creation that rebelled."

Hidden Mysteries and the Bible is for Christians of all backgrounds to use as a guidepost to current and future events. The prophet Daniel said that knowledge would increase in the end times. Here is the book that will increase the reader's knowledge and provide a condensed encyclopedia as a reference for a multitude of issues. As a gift, it is also an opportunity to open the evangelical door for discussions with unbelievers. Now is the time we need a fully integrated view of these topics to view the world as God intended us to understand from the words He gave us thousands of years ago. *Hidden Mysteries and the Bible* is a tool that helps us comprehend what lies before us and have an organized mindset to be able to influence others.

Don Mercer
Chairman of the Board, Prophecy Watchers Inc.
Author, *Rapture Mountain*
Lieutenant Colonel, US Army, Retired

Dr. Larry Ollison has an incredible anointing and gift of unraveling scriptures seldom discussed in-depth for a greater understanding of God's Word. *Hidden Mysteries and the Bible* is fascinating, riveting, revealing, and insightful.

Bill Koenig
Koenig World Watch Daily
http://watch.org

HIDDEN MYSTERIES

AND THE BIBLE

FOREWORD BY
RICK RENNER

HIDDEN
MYSTERIES
AND THE BIBLE

SECRETS REVEALED

ALIENS/UFOS, GIANTS,
TIME TRAVEL, MULTIVERSE,
AI & OTHER UNEXPLAINED
PHENOMENA

LARRY OLLISON, PH.D.

Published by Harrison House Publishers

Shippensburg, PA 17257

ISBN 13 TP: 978-1-6675-0298-4

ISBN 13 HC: 978-1-6675-0343-1

ISBN 13 eBook: 978-1-6675-0299-1

For Worldwide Distribution, Printed in the U.S.A.

1 2 3 4 5 6 7 8 / 28 27 26 25 24

CONTENTS

Foreword by Rick Renner xi

Preface xiii

Chapter One   Are We Alone? 1

Chapter Two   In the Beginning 19

Chapter Three   The World Before Adam and Eve 39

Chapter Four   The Watchers and the Nephilim 59

Chapter Five   Who Built the Ancient Structures? 89

Chapter Six   Angels of God 109

Chapter Seven   UFOs and the Bible 131

Chapter Eight   Time Travel 153

Chapter Nine   Artificial Intelligence and the Coming
Apocalypse 173

Chapter Ten   Transhumanism, Cryonics, and Eternal
Life 195

Chapter Eleven   Flat Earth Theory 209

Chapter Twelve   Ghosts 217

Chapter Thirteen   What Is the Multiverse? 229

Chapter Fourteen   Climate Change 237

Chapter Fifteen   Heaven, Hell, and Eternity 243

Chapter Sixteen   The Mystery of the Hebrew Language 263

Epilogue 279

Bibliography 281

About the Author 283

FOREWORD

Dr. Larry Ollison contacted me to see if I would be interested in writing the Foreword to this amazing book. My habit is that after I am requested to write either an Endorsement or a Foreword for a book, I first read it to see if it is one I want to endorse. After reading this manuscript, I am so glad that Larry asked for my involvement! This book is fascinating, intriguing, and it is packed full of answers for which people want answers!

In *Hidden Mysteries and the Bible*, Dr. Ollison takes a deep dive into the questions people want to ask, but do not know who to ask or who to trust for reliable answers. Although not every topic raised in this book can be answered with absolute certainty, Dr. Ollison has done his best to address each one. And where he could not provide a rock-solid answer, he directs readers on how to proceed deeper to find more information if they wish to do so. This book is a fabulous tool and one that readers will want to share with others!

I am a voracious reader of many kinds of books, but I found that this one, in addition to being packed with remarkable information, is written in a style that makes it one of the most enjoyable books I have read in a long time, and one I'm sure will captivate any reader. There may be parts of it you agree with, parts that make you ponder, and other parts that make you question—but, for sure, *this book will make you think!*

I'm so thankful Dr. Ollison asked me to read his book, review it, and write this Foreword for it. After reading every page of this manuscript, I can tell you that this is a book that is easy to read, and one you will not want to put down until you've read it to the end!

RICK RENNER
Minister, Author, Broadcaster
Moscow, Russia

PREFACE

I was raised in a family that always attended church. For that I am very thankful. I believe it is extremely important for children to be raised with belief in God and His Son, Jesus. As a child, I was taught the basic gospel of salvation and was told the supernatural stories of the Bible. However, I also was interested in science, astronomy, and archeology, and this began a lifelong quest to resolve the conflict between what I heard in Sunday School and what I heard in public school.

When science said the earth was old, and archeology was finding structures that were constructed tens of thousands of years in the past, I asked my Sunday School teachers why that disagreed with what I was taught in Sunday School. When astronomers discovered that our sun was only one of hundreds of thousands of stars in the Milky Way Galaxy, and that our galaxy was only one of billions of galaxies, my Sunday School teachers had no answers. All they could say was, "Larry, someday when you get to heaven, you can ask Jesus." That response was very unsatisfying. As a young student, waiting until I got to heaven seemed like an eternity away.

During my high school and university years, scientific discoveries and man's understanding of the universe and physics were progressing at an extremely rapid rate. For millennia, scientific understanding had increased at a snail's pace, but now each day brought new discoveries and revelation.

My search for answers took me to a place of frustration. Then one night I had a dream. The dream was quite detailed, but the essence of it was this: Without asking, God gave me the answers to all my questions about the universe and the supernatural, and the answers were quite simple. Although I didn't remember the answers when I woke up, the peace that came was overwhelming. I knew that my mysteries were not mysteries to God.

As the years have passed, I made a striking discovery. God's Word contains the answers to everything. Through misinterpretation of the Bible, lack of study, and religious tradition, many people experience frustration because of the perceived conflict between science and what the Bible teaches. Actually the Bible contains all knowledge and all wisdom and does not conflict with the physics that were created by God Himself. This true understanding eliminates confusion and brings peace.

In this book, *Hidden Mysteries and the Bible*, we will examine some historical, scientific, and religious issues that have raised questions through the centuries, as well as many contemporary issues, and compare them with the Bible. In making this comparison, we will discover that the Bible has a strong grasp of these issues. The Creator Himself tells us much in His Word.

A Christian will no longer have to vaguely answer people's questions but can strongly show that the Bible, the Holy Word of God, goes far beyond the science of today and reveals our ancient past and our distant future. The answers will eliminate confusion, bring peace, and strengthen faith in the God of the universe who sent His Son to redeem mankind.

Author's Note

Throughout this book there are references to "man" and "mankind." At the time of many Bible translations, it was commonly understood these terms referred to all of humanity, not just the male gender. But as culture and language usage have changed, let it be understood that in this book where references to "man" and "mankind" are used, I am referring to all of humanity.

Chapter One

ARE WE ALONE?

In the 1997 science fiction classic film *Contact,* based on the 1985 novel written by Carl Sagan, a young Ellie Arroway (played by Jodie Foster) looked at the stars through a telescope and asked her father, "Dad, do you think there's people on other planets?" He said to her, "I don't know, Sparks. But I guess I'd say if it is just us…seems like an awful waste of space." In other words, Ellie was asking, "Are we alone?"

This question is the root of all the mysteries of mankind. Are we alone? Is there something or someone beyond our ability to see, understand, or even comprehend?

Humanity, the earth, and all that exists is obviously not an accident or a random happening. To understand the vastness of the universe, the endlessness of time—future and past—stretches the comprehension of man beyond the ability to grasp. As knowledge has begun to rapidly increase, man is losing the ability to assimilate or fully understand the knowledge he is obtaining. It's overwhelming!

Several years ago, while talking to a National Aeronautics and Space Administration (NASA) scientist who worked on the Apollo 8 program, I was told that it would take several years (with the computing systems they had back then) to process data concerning the universe that NASA had already collected. I'm sure that in the years since then, with the rapid increase in computing power, this statement is no longer accurate. However, according to NASA's own website, it wasn't until 2019 that nine teams were selected to study rocks from the moon mission that had been carefully stored and left untouched for nearly 50 years.

But with all this accumulated knowledge, mankind is still asking the same question, "Are we alone?"

Do You Believe in God?

Recently, a world-renowned scientist was interviewed concerning the cosmos and the beginning of the universe. In his interview, the host asked the question, "Do you believe in God?" The scientist's response was that he did not believe in a god as most world religions taught; but considering the complexity of the universe and the intricacies of how every part coordinated, there is no way it could have happened randomly. When pressed about the question of God's existence, he re-emphasized that he did not believe in the God of the Bible but acknowledged that there must be some force that keeps everything in order.

In his intellect and depth of thinking, while denying faith in a god, he proclaimed there must be an intelligence somewhere that organized all that we see and all that we don't see. In his denial of there being a god, he inadvertently proclaimed there is one. Although some great men of science deny the existence of God, they do admit to some type of intelligent design, but they offer no alternative.

Intelligent Design

When I was young, I watched the voyages of *Star Trek* on television. Space travel seemed so easy. To travel great distances, all we needed was to tell Chekov to put it in warp drive. With our limited knowledge of space in the 1960s, this type of space travel seemed somewhat plausible. But within a short time, we began to realize the unimaginable immenseness of space—the size and scale is impossible to comprehend.

In the universe that we can see, there are two trillion galaxies, and we know that is not all of them. The galaxy that contains our solar system, the Milky Way, is not very large compared to other galaxies, but it has over one hundred billion stars in it. With light traveling at 186,282 miles per second, it would take more than 100,000 years for light to travel from one side of the Milky Way to the other, and this is just one galaxy among the two trillion that we know of.

As telescopes in space increase their view beyond what we can now see, the question becomes even more relevant. Are we alone? Or more precisely, is it even possible that we could be alone? Are there alien beings on other planets somewhere in another galaxy, or possibly in another universe? Are there beings very close to us only in a different dimension?

With recent archeological discoveries, advancements in technology, and artificial intelligence developments, new questions have come to light. While many theologians believe that the earth is only 6,000 years old, how do we resolve the discoveries of ancient artifacts dating back many millennia? Has the earth been visited before by someone other than humans? Is it possible for mechanical beings made by man to become sentient? Would it be possible for man to become their slaves and no longer the master of the technology he created? Through medical science, can life be extended indefinitely?

There is a source of wisdom and knowledge that is beyond the natural knowledge of man. Man can only manipulate and rearrange substances that already exist in order to design or develop mechanics or medicine. But all of this must be done with materials that have already been created and with the laws of physics that already exist. The substance and the physics of the dimension man lives in could not have developed out of nothing. Science agrees that nothing can be created from nothing.

So is there an intelligent design to everything that we see? The answer is yes! And that intelligence is in the mind of God. Other than Jehovah God, there is no other candidate for this intelligence. Those who oppose "intelligent design by God" have no other realistic option or source of intelligence to present. If everything created, both seen and unseen, was created and designed by this intelligence that we know as God, then it stands to reason that He knows the answers to all our seemingly simplistic questions.

Comparing our intelligence to His could be considered humorous because of the vastness of the difference in our intellect.

Who has measured the waters in the hollow of His hand, measured heaven with a span and calculated the dust of the earth in a measure? Weighed the mountains in scales and the hills in a balance? Who has directed the Spirit of the LORD, or as His counselor has taught Him? With whom did He take counsel, and who instructed Him, and taught Him in the path of justice? Who taught Him knowledge, and showed Him the way of understanding?

ISAIAH 40:12-14

Our Limited Understanding

When my daughter was four years old, I was leaving for the office one day when she asked me where I was going. On that particular day I was meeting with some employees about their duties, meeting with a tax accountant to discuss my taxes, and dropping off my car for a minor repair. For me to explain to my daughter the federal tax system and how it affected my income, or for me to explain the complexities of the duties of the employees, or to detail the problems and solutions concerning my automobile repair would have been ludicrous. She would never have understood even a simplification of these details.

So as she stood at the door, I simply said, "I'm leaving and have some things to take care of, but I'll be home for dinner." She was satisfied with my answer to her question and went happily about her day.

Much in the same way, as advanced as our knowledge has become, we are still like a four-year-old child standing at the door compared to the complexity of God. God's thoughts are higher than our thoughts. But for the children who just need to know more, He did give us a Book that can reveal the deep things of God.

> *For as the heavens are higher than the earth, so are My ways higher than your ways, and My thoughts than your thoughts.*
>
> Isaiah 55:9

With all these questions, it would seem there is no easy answer. But in searching for answers, a decision must be made. Will we look to the Book the Creator gave us, or will we rely on our own mental assumptions derived from the technology of our own creation? There can only be one answer. We must seek the wisdom behind the intelligent design, which is God and His Word He has given us.

This Ancient Book sheds light on our past and our future and gives answers to these difficult questions. The God of all existence has given us His Manual. Within this Book, He has given us revelation by the Holy Spirit—the Spirit of God Himself. That book is the Word of God, the Holy Bible.

> *Sanctify them by Your truth. Your word is truth.*
>
> John 17:17

Within the Word of God, all truth is contained. The mysteries of man, the universe, and multiple dimensions may appear as mysteries to man's understanding, but within the mind of God there is no mystery.

No Beginning, No End, and No Mystery

In the beginning, God created everything we see and everything we don't see. The visible and the invisible surround us, and it was all created by the Supreme Being we know as Almighty God.

But before this world was created, and before time began, God existed without beginning. Our Creator was not created but has existed eternally. It is impossible to write His autobiography because there was never a starting point for His existence. This reality alone is beyond the comprehension of man. Because of His incomprehensible existence and power, the finite mind of man will never fully understand the infinite mind of God.

In countless articles and sermons, I have heard the Bible quoted, often being used as an excuse as to why we don't understand the mysteries of our universe. First Corinthians 2:9 is often quoted: "Eye has not seen, nor ear heard, nor have entered into the heart of man the things which God has prepared for those who love Him." Sadly, they stop there and follow with a statement of how we can never understand what God has prepared for us. If they would only continue to the next verse, they would see that the mysteries of God are revealed to us by God Himself through His Holy Spirit. Verse 10 says, "But **God has revealed them to us through His Spirit**. For the Spirit searches all things, yes, the deep things of God."

The world is full of unsolved mysteries and conspiracy theories. How do we know what to believe? How do we know the truth? How can we attain peace in the midst of conflicting ideas? Is there a way to solve these unexplained mysteries and have peace in our hearts, knowing that the answers are available through the revelation of God's Word by the Holy Spirit?

The Miracle of the Bible

The Holy Bible is a supernatural book inspired by the Holy Spirit and written by 40 authors over thousands of years. It is compiled seamlessly into one edition with one theme and one purpose. It is truly a miracle. This begins with the writings of Moses and continues with the writings of prophets that press through the cultures of past ages, using the Septuagint translation, the Latin Vulgate, and ultimately resulting in the canon of Scriptures we have now.

Countless volumes of history could be written on the transformation, translation, martyrs, and victories of the past that brought us to the complete Word of God that we have today. But the bottom line is this: The world has the complete and uncompromised Book on the earth today that God has supernaturally prepared through the inspiration of His Holy Spirit for mankind to have as a Manual in the end of days.

> *The grass withers, the flower fades, but the word of our God stands forever.*
>
> Isaiah 40:8

Although it is one book, it is divided into two sections that we call the Old Testament and the New Testament. The word *testament* could be more clearly understood as contract or covenant. The Britannica Dictionary defines *testament* as "proof or evidence that something exists or is true."

Of course, we know that the Bible was not written all at once, but composed, compiled, and molded into the final publication over centuries. The original Scriptures penned by Moses are what we now call *The Torah* or *The Pentateuch*. *Pentateuch* is a Greek word that simply means *five*. This refers to the first five books of the Bible—Genesis, Exodus, Leviticus, Numbers, and Deuteronomy. As time passed, other historical Jewish writings by the prophets and kings were added.

Other Ancient Manuscripts

The biblical principles expressed throughout this book, *Hidden Mysteries and the Bible*, are based on the nuggets of truth within the Holy Scriptures. From time to time, references will be made to other ancient writings. Some of these will be books referred to within the Holy Scriptures, and others are from manuscripts discovered in the Dead Sea Scrolls. However, they will be used to supplement and complement the Scriptures and never directly contradict them.

Throughout history there have been books and documents written that have contained truth, commentary, and opinion. Some people consider these writings to be so accurate that they almost elevate them to the level of Scripture. While some writings have been canonized by certain Christian groups, other groups have rejected the same manuscripts. Needless to say, with these writings there is great controversy. They fall into different categories that sometimes overlap. But whether they are pseudepigraphal, apocryphal, or testaments of the patriarchs, etc., they are not considered to be on the level of canonized Scripture.

The Dead Sea Scrolls

Sometime between November 1946 and February 1947, three Bedouin shepherds discovered seven scrolls housed in jars in a cave near Qumran, Israel. They took a handful of scrolls (that included the Isaiah scroll and the Habakkuk commentary) back to the camp to show their family. Thankfully, none of the scrolls were destroyed in the process. The Bedouins kept these scrolls hanging on a tent pole, periodically taking them to display to their tribe.

They tried to sell the scrolls to a dealer in Bethlehem, but he returned them, saying they were worthless. He said this because he feared they might have been stolen from a synagogue. Undaunted by this, the shepherds went to a market and found a Syrian Christian who offered to buy them. The original scrolls changed hands, and some were sold for very low prices.

The rediscovery of the Qumran caves started in 1949 by the Jordanian Department of Antiquities. Since then, several other caves have been discovered with a total of 972 manuscripts having been found. About 40 percent of the documents are copies of texts from Hebrew Scriptures. Another 30 percent are texts from the second temple period, which were not canonized in the Hebrew Bible. This includes the Book of Enoch, the Book of Jubilees, the Book of Tobit, the Wisdom of Sirach, Psalms 152-155, and several others. The remaining 30 percent of the scrolls are manuscripts of previously unknown documents that shed light on the rules of groups within Judaism.

The following is a brief definition of these non-canonized books.

Pseudepigrapha

Pseudepigrapha is defined as Jewish writings ascribed to various biblical patriarchs and prophets. Examples would be the *Book of Adam*, *The Assumption of Moses*, *Melchizedek*, *The Ascension of Isaiah*, and *The Wisdom of Sirach*.

Pseudepigraphal books were written from 300 BC to AD 300. They were not included in the Septuagint and are rarely regarded as inspired Scripture. Although they connect with biblical figures, many times they are not verifiable by the canonized Bible. An example of this is the book, *The Apocalypse of Adam*, where Adam had a vision and related it to his son, Seth.

Many scholars also use the term to describe later books allegedly written by New Testament characters. Some claim these "gnostic gospels" were written by Thomas, Peter, and other New Testament figures.

There are examples of canonized biblical Scripture that some consider pseudepigrapha. One such example in the New Testament is the book of Second Peter. Many scholars believe the book of Second Peter was written 80 years after the apostle Peter's death. The book is thought to be written from known statements, writings, and documents by Peter and compiled by an unknown person but attributed to Peter.

Apocrypha

Apocrypha is defined as biblically related writings that are not accepted as canonized Scripture because they are not considered genuine by some scholars.

The apocryphal books were written between 400 BC and AD 1. This is the same time period between the last book of the Old Testament (Malachi) and the birth of Jesus. The Apocrypha was included in the Septuagint (the Greek translation of the Old Testament), and despite Jerome's objections was included in the Vulgate (Latin) Bible.

The Roman Catholic Church and the Eastern Orthodox Church regard the Apocrypha as Scripture. Many Protestants consider it a useful resource but definitely not part of the holy canonized Scriptures. Even Martin Luther was known for saying that these books are not considered equal to the Holy Scriptures, but they are useful and good to read.

There are times when it appears that some New Testament authors quote from these books. Jude appears to quote from *The Testament of Moses* and Jude 1:14-15 includes a saying from *The Book of Enoch*. No major Christian denomination considers the pseudepigrapha as inspired Scripture. Examples of pseudepigraphical writings are:

- *The Apocalypse of Abraham*
- *The Books of Adam and Eve*
- *The Apocalypse of Adam*
- *The Book of Enoch*
- *The Fourth Book of Ezra*

- *The Book of Giants*
- *The Book of Jubilees*
- *The Lives of the Prophets*
- *The Testament of Moses*
- *The Testaments of the Sons of Jacob*
- *The Gospel of Mary*
- *The Gospel of Nicodemus*
- *The Gospel of Thomas*
- *The Gospel of Barnabas*
- and more.

While these books contain some insight, there are many historical facts scattered throughout them that are not accurate or that contradict biblical history.

In recent years, there have been several novels written (such as *The Da Vinci Code*) that use material in these non-canonized gnostic gospels to weave an interesting conspiracy story. However, despite this they are still not considered Scripture and there is little debate on this subject by theologians or scholars.

The bottom line is this: The Holy Bible we have today containing 39 Old Testament books and 27 New Testament books has stood the test of time and is the only true reference for truth. The New Testament was officially canonized at the Synod of Hippo in AD 393. Other writings, whether pseudepigraphal or apocryphal, may be used for reference and study. Some may be authentic while others may not; however, they should only be considered worthy when the text parallels and does not conflict with the Holy Bible.

Translating the Bible

When translating the meaning of one language into another, oftentimes minor mistakes are made that can dramatically change the meaning intended by the author. While a superficial reading seems correct, a more thorough investigation can sometimes yield a different result.

Before we go any further, we must understand the difference between translation, transliteration, and interpretation.

Translation is changing the words of one language (Hebrew/Greek) into the words of another language (English), and the words have the same meaning.

Transliteration is simply taking the letters in a word of one language (Hebrew/Greek) and converting them into the corresponding letters of another language (English), thus creating a new word in the second language. Unfortunately, sometimes the new transliterated word is given a new meaning that conflicts with the original word.

For example, if we transliterate the Greek word *angelos*, taking the Greek letters and converting them into the English equivalent, it gives us the English word *angels*. However, the Greek word *angelos* has meanings other than angel, such as messenger, envoy, or one who is sent. So, we can see that the word *angelos* must be translated according to the context. As an example, *angelos* is referring to an angel that appeared to Peter in prison (Acts 12:7) but *angelos* refers to a human messenger in John's vision in Revelation 22:8-9.

Interpretation is reading a passage in one language and rephrasing it in another language based upon the understanding of the person doing the interpretation. There are Bibles that are paraphrased. That simply means the manuscript is read and rephrased according to the way the scholar perceives the meaning of the original manuscript.

With this in mind, much confusion and wrong beliefs have occurred in the church because of misinterpretation, mistranslation, or transliteration. So, many times we refer back to the original language to determine the original intent of the writer.

Three Basic Biblical Principles

As we examine historical and future events, there are some basic biblical principles that must be addressed. Without an understanding of these principles, there will be confusion and misunderstanding.

1. Three Groups of People on Earth

We must understand that, according to Scripture, there are three groups of people currently living on earth (1 Corinthians 10:31-32). Everyone born in this current dispensation (church age) is either a Jew or a Gentile. When they become a born-again Christian, they are no longer a Jew or a Gentile, but become a member of a new group called the church (2 Corinthians 5:17). The reason this must be understood is quite simple. The path for each of the three groups throughout history and into the future is not the same.

All Scripture does not apply to everyone, so it must be interpreted in context. While we are told in the New Testament that all Scripture is profitable for the church for doctrine, reproof, correction, and teaching (2 Timothy 3:16), every Scripture is not *to* the church. If you attempt to interpret specific promises that are made to the church and apply them to the Jews, it will bring confusion. Or if you attempt to take a scripture that was written to the Jews and apply it to the church or to the Gentiles, it will bring confusion and incorrect beliefs.

A simple example would be 1 Thessalonians 4:15-18, which is a prophecy of a future event for the church. It says the dead in Christ will rise first, then we who are living will be caught up together with them in the clouds. This is not referring to nonbelieving Jews or Gentiles, but only to the church. Likewise, when the Bible promises that Jerusalem and the land of Israel will be given to the righteous Jews, that promise is not for the Gentiles or the church. Each of the three groups has its individual promises and future timeline.

We must rightly divide the Word; and of course, if it can be rightly divided, it can also be wrongly divided (2 Timothy 2:15).

2. Spirit, Soul, and Body

Mankind was created by God as a three-part being—spirit, soul, and body (1 Thessalonians 5:23). Although we are made up of three parts, there are scriptures that refer specifically to our body while others refer specifically to our spirit or soul. An example of this is when the dead in Christ are resurrected from the earth at the rapture of the church. Their spirit and soul are already in heaven and will return with Jesus to be reunited with their body that is in the grave (or wherever). Once again, there can be confusion if we do not understand the difference between the spirit, soul, and body.

Simply put, we are a created spirit being that possesses a soul (mind, will, intellect, and emotions) and lives within a body. When non-believers receive Jesus as Lord and Savior, their spirit man is born again, but their soul and body are not. Their spirit is then living eternally, and their citizenship is in heaven, but their body is still living on the earth and continuing to age.

3. The Seen and Unseen Worlds

There are two worlds—two different dimensions—existing simultaneously and parallel to each other. One is physical, one is spiritual. The Bible calls the physical world the "world of the seen" and the spiritual world "the world of the unseen."

> *While we do not look at the things which are seen, but at the things which are not seen. For the things which are seen are temporary, but the things which are not seen are eternal.*
>
> 2 CORINTHIANS 4:18

While these two worlds are separate, they do interact and there are portals of travel between the two. Everything in the world that is seen was created by the world that is not seen (Hebrews 11:3). There are times when the Holy Scriptures refer to these two worlds as the heavenly realm and the earthly realm (Matthew 18:18).

Faith helps us understand that God created the whole world by his command. This means that the things we see were made by something that cannot be seen.

Hebrews 11:3 ERV

When we understand that the Word of God is the ultimate truth and there is no error in the divine writings that were inspired by the Holy Spirit, then as we look at the creation scriptures, truths we've never seen before begin to unfold.

Are We Alone?

All the mysteries and questions that arise cannot be answered until we answer this one question: "Are we alone?" Is there another entity who is guiding us through our history and imparting knowledge as we are able to comprehend it? Is there a Creator overseeing mankind or has He assigned supernatural beings to help guide us? It is ludicrous to think that everything we see is a result of the miraculous rearranging of space dust. We must acknowledge this: We are not alone.

There is a Creator and there are multiple dimensions. There is the world we live in that we see and possibly multiple unknown worlds that we don't yet see.

So when we ask the question, "Are we alone?" the answer is obvious. NO! We are not alone.

Chapter Two

In the Beginning

My Christian background is very conservative. I grew up in a Christian home where we attended church regularly, and I became a Christian at an early age. From those early years I was taught to check everything out with the Word of God, the Holy Bible. If the Bible said it, I believed it. Because of this, I have altered much of my theology and views to align with the Bible several times over the years. We should never have an opinion and try to prove it by taking scriptures out of context. Rather, we should take the sum of the scriptures and align our thinking and beliefs with them.

In my studies, I discovered there are many views concerning creation. Science seemed to be the standard that was used to prove or discredit the Bible. But the truth is, true science and the Bible do not conflict. The Word of God never evolves; however, the revelation of the Word increases as we approach the end of days. The prophet Daniel was told to seal up a scroll that was written and it would not be revealed until the end of days (Daniel 12:4). We are now in the end of days, and much is being revealed.

Shortly after Jesus placed His blood on the altar in heaven, the Holy Spirit was given as a gift to the church on the Day of Pentecost. The Holy Spirit, the Spirit of the living God, is the One who reveals Scripture (John 16:13) and brings to light revelation that has been hidden from previous generations. Scientific facts change, but the Word of God never changes. Jesus is the Word (John 1:1,14), and the Word never changes (Hebrews 13:8).

Medical science once thought that putting mercury into the bloodstream would kill certain sicknesses. It was later discovered that it was the mercury itself that killed many who were treated by these early doctors. Once again, scientific facts change, but the absolute foundational truth in the Word of God never changes. Revelation of Scripture, by the Holy Spirit, increases in the last days.

> But you, Daniel, shut up the words, and seal the book until the time of the end; many shall run to and fro, and knowledge shall increase.
>
> DANIEL 12:4

The knowledge that God has given mankind through science confirms the Word of God to be true. George Washington Carver was a great African American agriculturist and educator who received international acclaim for his amazing discoveries. As a strong Christian, Carver lived practicing his faith. In his walks in the woods, he would pray, and frequently asserted publicly that his insights for his discoveries came as a revelation from God.

As stated throughout this manuscript, there are some biblical beliefs that are *not* salvation critical. Young Earth versus Old Earth is one of those.

Young Earth Versus Old Earth

When it comes to the ancient past regarding the creation of the world and mankind, there are two basic Christian viewpoints: Young Earth Creationist and Old Earth Creationist. Neither of these two groups believe that mankind naturally evolved from space dust; but rather, that divine design was involved. Both groups believe that God the Father created everything by His Word, through His Word, and for His Word (Colossians 1:16). The difference is this: Did it happen in six 24-hour periods, or did it happen through the eons of time?

The most traditional interpretation of the creation of the earth is the literal view of the first chapter of Genesis. That interpretation says everything we see within our universe was created in six 24-hour days. Generally speaking, with small variations, this is the Young Earth view of creation.

A second general view that is more controversial, and even considered to be heresy by some denominations, is that Genesis chapter 1 is only an overview of creation. The details, however, are in chronological order. This chapter in Genesis spans a greater amount of time than six literal days and reveals what we need to know about our past and who the Creator is.

The Young Earth Creationist view follows the strict literal interpretation of Genesis 1; therefore, it needs no interpretation.

With that in mind, let's take a look at the Old Earth view of creation and what the first chapter of Genesis says.

Bara Elohim—God Created

Genesis, the Hebrew book of beginnings, starts by saying, "In the beginning God created the heavens and the earth."

It's good to note *the beginning* referenced here is not the beginning of God, His existence, His habitation, or His purpose. His existence has no beginning and cannot be measured by any timing device because He lives outside the framework of time. *"In the beginning"* is referring to the time of beginnings for humankind. The knowledge of the existence of God before that moment could not be contained in the memory of all the computer storage on earth. Actually, it is impossible for us to even comprehend.

The phrase "God created" is *bara elohim* in Hebrew. *Elohim* is plural. If the word for *God* in this phrase is plural, then who is it referring to? It is referring to God the Father, God the Son, and God the Holy Spirit.

In John chapter 1, verses 1 and 3, the apostle John wrote, "In the beginning was the Word, and the Word was with God, and the Word was God. ...All things were made through Him, and without Him nothing was made that was made." Then in verse 14, John makes this astonishing statement: "The Word became flesh and dwelt among us...." He was definitely referring to Jesus, so Jesus was in the beginning, the Father was in the beginning, and as we see in Genesis 1:2, the Spirit of

God hovered over the waters. So, in the beginning God—the Father, Son, Holy Spirit—created the heavens and the earth.

Jesus spoke of this when praying shortly before His crucifixion. He said, "And now, O Father, glorify Me together with Yourself, with the glory which I had with You **before the world was**" (John 17:5).

God Created the Heavens

Some translations of the Bible translate the word *heavens* as singular. However, the Hebrew word *hashamayim* in the original text is plural. God created the *heavens*. How many heavens are there? The apostle Paul, speaking of himself in the third person, said that he went into the third heaven, and in the third heaven was the Paradise of God.

> *I know a man in Christ who fourteen years ago— whether in the body I do not know, or whether out of the body I do not know, God knows—such a one was caught up to the third heaven. ...how he was caught up into Paradise....*
>
> 2 CORINTHIANS 12:2,4

The Testament of Levi states there are seven heavens. Who was Levi and why should his writings matter? The father of Levi was Jacob whose name was changed to Israel (Genesis 32:28). Jacob's father was Isaac, and Isaac's father was Abraham. Levi is the great-grandson of Abraham.

The custom of the day was for the patriarchs, such as Levi, to write a testament of their wisdom and knowledge to be given to their children before their passing. Certainly Levi, given who the members of his family were, would have acquired great knowledge.

The Testament of Levi was found in the Dead Sea Scrolls in the twentieth century. In his testament, he said there were seven heavens, which he describes. Regardless of whether there are three heavens, seven heavens or more, God created them all.

How Big Are the Heavens?

This brings us to another question. How large is the expanse of the heavens? As stated earlier, current astronomers estimate that there are two trillion (2,000 billion) known galaxies in our universe. Each of these galaxies contain hundreds of thousands of stars. One of these galaxies is the Milky Way in which our star (the sun) rotates. For light to travel across the Milky Way Galaxy, from one side to the other, would take more than 100 thousand years.

When God created the heavens, it was no small thing. The Bible goes on to say that when He created the heavens, He also created the earth. Isaiah 45:18 says that God did not create the earth *tohu* (desolate), but He created it to be inhabited—completely ready for mankind.

> *For thus says the LORD, who created the heavens (he is God!), who formed the earth and made it (he established it; he did not create it empty, he formed it to be inhabited!): "I am the LORD, and there is no other."*
> Isaiah 45:18 ESV

The Days of Re-Creation

God created the heavens and the earth before the first Day, and they were created perfect to be inhabited by man. But in verse 2 (again, before the first Day), the earth was in chaos (Hebrew—*tohu*) and flooded, and it needed to be put back in order.

This original flood (brought on by Satan being cast to the earth with his fallen angels because of their rebellion) should not be confused with the flood of Noah that happened 1,656 years after Adam and Eve were cast out of the Garden of Eden. The first flood—before the days of re-creation—I call the Luciferian Flood.

> *In the beginning God created the heavens and the earth. The earth was without form, and void; and darkness was on the face of the deep. And the Spirit of God was hovering over the face of the waters.*
> GENESIS 1:1-2

First Day

On Day 1, in the midst of darkness and chaos, the reconstruction process began. God said, "Let there be light," or more correctly, He said, "Light be," and there was light. (The original translation of the Hebrew is "Light be.") God was the Light of Day 1.

> *Then God said, "Let there be light"; and there was light. And God saw the light, that it was good; and*

God divided the light from the darkness. God called the
light Day, and the darkness He called Night.
So the evening and the morning were the first day.

GENESIS 1:3-5

While some may see this as difficult to comprehend, think outside the box with me for a moment. God is light and in Him is no darkness at all (1 John 1:5). After the world He created to be inhabited became formless and void with darkness and water over the face of the deep, God stood in the middle of the darkness and proclaimed that He was there. When God arrived, the darkness had to leave. He is the Light.

This light cannot be referring to the sun and the moon because they were not revealed until Day 4. The Bible does not say that God created day and night on the first day. Day and night already existed as the earth, its rotation, and the solar system were already there. He simply named the light Day and He named the darkness Night. This was Day 1.

What was created on Day 1? Nothing. What already existed was separated and named.

Second Day

Then on Day 2, God said, "Let there be an expanse in the midst of the waters, and let it separate the waters from the waters" (Genesis 1:6 ESV). He made the firmament (the first heaven and earth's atmosphere) by separating the waters. He named the expanse Heaven.

What did He create on Day 2? Actually nothing. He separated the waters that were already there. Remember, the water was already on the earth in verse 2 (before Day 1). So, the water was not created on Day 2. The waters already existed, and He just separated them, making the atmosphere (firmament).

> *Then God said, "Let there be a firmament in the midst of the waters, and let it divide the waters from the waters." Thus God made the firmament, and divided the waters which were under the firmament from the waters which were above the firmament; and it was so. And God called the firmament Heaven.*
>
> *So the evening and the morning were the second day.*
>
> Genesis 1:6-8

Third Day

On Day 3, God separated the waters so that dry land could appear. God named (called) the dry land Earth, and the waters He called Seas. Remember in verse one the earth was created perfect. The water to make the Seas was created in the beginning (before the first day) but separated into Seas on Day 3.

> *Then God said, "Let the waters under the heavens be gathered together into one place, and let the dry land appear"; and it was so. And God called the dry land Earth, and the gathering together of the waters He called Seas. And God saw that it was good.*
>
> Genesis 1:9-10

Then God said, "Let the earth bring forth grass, the herb that yields seed, and the fruit tree that yields fruit according to its kind, **whose seed is in itself on the earth**; and it was so" (verse 11). Where did that seed come from? According to the Bible, it was in the earth from a time before the earth was covered with water.

What was created on Day 3? Again, nothing. Waters that already existed were gathered together and vegetation grew from seed that was already in the earth. Could it be that this seed was the seed left over from the earth before the Luciferian flood, which covered the earth before Day 1 of creation?

> *Then God said, "Let the earth bring forth grass, the herb that yields seed, and the fruit tree that yields fruit according to its kind, whose seed is in itself, on the earth"; and it was so. And the earth brought forth grass, the herb that yields seed according to its kind, and the tree that yields fruit, whose seed is in itself according to its kind. And God saw that it was good.*
>
> *So the evening and the morning were the third day.*
>
> Genesis 1:11-13

It has been shown that seed can remain viable under certain conditions for thousands of years. There was a group of Israelis who found seed in a cannister in Egypt that was more than 4,000 years old. They took it back to Israel (everything grows in Israel), planted it, and grew wheat from the 4,000-year-old seed. Seed can carry life within itself for a long time.

On one trip to Israel, I talked with two elderly rabbis who believed that the seed spoken of in the Torah (on Day 3 of creation) was already in the earth. Obviously, the world that existed before the waters covered the earth had plant life that was destroyed by the flood, but the seed remained on the earth.

Fourth Day

On Day 4, God acknowledged the lights in the expanse of the heavens that He had already declared to separate the day and the night. He stated that they would be for signs, for seasons, and for days and years and that they would give light upon the earth. Verse 16 in Genesis 1 says that God made two great lights—the sun and the moon. Notice it says that God *made* two great lights. It does not say that God *created* them. They already existed in the original heavens and earth.

A good example of the difference between *making* and *creating* is this: A carpenter can make a chair using wood. However, he doesn't create the wood. The wood already existed, and he fashioned the chair using wood that had already been created.

Likewise, God revealed the lights (sun, moon, and stars) in such a way that they could be clearly visible. Previously they were obstructed by waters that were in the firmament (atmosphere). Again, it was the fine-tuning, repairing, and re-establishing the conditions on the earth that existed before the destruction that took place between verse 1 and verse 2 (and before Day 1). And that was the fourth day.

> *Then God said, "Let there be lights in the firmament of the heavens to divide the day from the night; and let them be for signs and seasons, and for days and years; and let them be for lights in the firmament of the heavens to give light on the earth"; and it was so.*

Then God made two great lights: the greater light to rule the day, and the lesser light to rule the night. He made the stars also. God set them in the firmament of the heavens to give light on the earth, and to rule over the day and over the night, and to divide the light from the darkness. And God saw that it was good.

So the evening and the morning were the fourth day.

GENESIS 1:14-19

Fifth Day

On Day 5, the earth was ready for God to create living beings to inhabit the earth. He created fish, great sea creatures, and all the living creatures that swim in the waters, and birds to fill the skies.

An interesting note here is that God wanted them to reproduce according to their own kind. Hybrids do not seem to be within God's plan. And with that creation, the fifth day ended.

Then God said, "Let the waters abound with an abundance of living creatures, and let birds fly above the earth across the face of the firmament of the heavens." So God created great sea creatures and every living thing that moves, with which the waters abounded, according to their kind, and every winged bird according to its kind.

And God saw that it was good. And God blessed them, saying, "Be fruitful and multiply, and fill the waters in the seas, and let birds multiply on the earth."

So the evening and the morning were the
fifth day.

GENESIS 1:20-23

Sixth Day

On Day 6, the tame animals, wild animals, and reptiles were created. Again, they were to reproduce according to their kind. God looked at what He had done and said it was good.

Then God said, "Let the earth bring forth the living
creature according to its kind: cattle and creeping thing
and beast of the earth, each according to its kind";
and it was so. And God made the beast of the earth
according to its kind, cattle according to its kind, and
everything that creeps on the earth according to its
kind. And God saw that it was good.

GENESIS 1:24-25

This brings us to the last and final creation on the earth. God said it was time to "'make humans, and they will be like us. We will let them rule the fish, the birds, and all other living creatures.' So, God created humans to be like himself; He made men and women," and He blessed them (Genesis 1:26-27 CEV).

Then God said, "Let Us make man in Our image,
according to Our likeness; let them have dominion over
the fish of the sea, over the birds of the air, and over the
cattle, over all the earth and over every creeping thing
that creeps on the earth."

So God created man in His own image; in the image of God He created him; male and female He created them. Then God blessed them, and God said to them, "Be fruitful and multiply; fill the earth and subdue it; have dominion over the fish of the sea, over the birds of the air, and over every living thing that moves on the earth."

Genesis 1:26-28

Chapter 2 of Genesis gives a more detailed account of the creation of Adam and Eve, which lends credence to the thought that chapter 1 is more of an overview rather than an exact detailed account. In fact, in Genesis 1, Adam and Eve are not even named (Genesis 1:27); they were just called male and female. After God blessed them, He commanded them to be fruitful and multiply and fill the earth and subdue it and have dominion (dominate) over every living thing on the earth.

And the sixth day was completed.

...So the evening and the morning were the sixth day.

Genesis 1:31

Seventh Day

Thus the heavens and the earth, and all the host of them, were finished. And on the seventh day God ended His work which He had done, and He rested on the seventh day from all His work which He had done. Then God blessed the seventh day and sanctified it, because in it He rested from all His work which God had created and made.

Genesis 2:1-3

God creates structure before it's needed. He created Eden before He created Adam. He created the earth before He created the animals, and the atmosphere before He created the birds. He completed His creation before He created man. God built the "house" before He placed man in it. After all creation was finished and after placing man in the Garden, He blessed him, and God said:

"See, I have given you every herb that yields seed which is on the face of all the earth, and every tree whose fruit yields seed; to you it shall be for food. Also, to every beast of the earth, to every bird of the air, and to everything that creeps on the earth, in which there is life, I have given every green herb for food"; and it was so.

Genesis 1:29-30

God gave man dominion over the earth and all that it contained. At that point, it became man's responsibility to tend and keep God's creation, and to obey God's instruction.

Then God rested from all His work which He had done (Genesis 2:2).

Adam and Eve—Literal or Allegorical?

Many theologians and seminaries teach the doctrine that Adam and Eve were not real human beings who were created by God and were not the parents of all living humanity. Rather, they say it is simply a story told in the Bible that generalized and represented the beginning of humanity. This doctrine goes deep into the heart of faith. Do we believe the Word of God or not?

To find the truth about this, we must go to the Book itself that contains the story of Adam and Eve and examine it for its relevance to salvation, forgiveness, and eternal life. There are many scriptures that verify that Adam and Eve were truly literal, physical human beings who were the beginning of all human ancestry.

In Luke's account of the birth of Jesus, he gives a detailed genealogy of Jesus' parents, grandparents, great-grandparents, etc. back to Seth, then to Seth's father, Adam. Luke was a physician who penned the Gospel of Luke in the New Testament and also the book of Acts. In his research, all of the ancestry of Jesus listed was literal with no fictional characters added as an illustration. To imply that the family tree detailed in the book of Luke is not accurate would likewise question the validity of the books of Luke and Acts.

Jesus shed His blood and placed it on the altar in heaven as the once-and-for-all act of redeeming man from sin. But what sin is He redeeming us from? Where in the Bible does it state that the sin of man entered into the earth, and that man lived with a sin nature as a result of this original sin?

Paul answered that question in Romans 5:12 where he wrote, "Therefore, **just as through one man sin entered the world,** and death through sin, and thus death spread to all men, because all sinned." Then verse 14 says that death reigned from Adam to Moses. Obviously, both Adam and Moses were living humans.

In Paul's letter to the Corinthians, he wrote that the first man (Adam) became a living being and the last Adam (referring to Jesus) became a life-giving spirit (1 Corinthians 15:45). He further tells us in 1 Corinthians 15:47 that the first man (referring to Adam) was made from the dust. But the second Man (referring to Jesus) was from heaven.

According to the New Testament authors, the apostles, and the early church fathers, there was no doubt Adam was a literal living human being created by God who was not a character in literature that simply represented the beginning of humanity. The Bible also says Adam was 930 years old when he died. If Adam were only a fictional character, the Bible would not have given the exact number of years he lived.

> *So all the days that Adam lived were nine hundred and thirty years; and he died.*
>
> GENESIS 5:5

However, the ultimate proof comes from a statement made by Jesus Himself in Mark 10:6. He said that in the beginning of creation, God made male and female—referring specifically to Adam and Eve. According to Genesis, Adam and Eve had three sons—Cain, Abel, and Seth. Cain murdered his brother Abel, and Jesus referred to that incident and to Abel specifically in Luke 11:51. He is referring to a real person, Abel, the son of Adam specifically by name.

*That on you may come all the righteous blood shed on the earth, **from the blood of righteous Abel** to the blood of Zechariah....*

Matthew 23:35

Without the literal sin of a literal man named Adam, there did not need to be the literal sacrifice and the literal blood of Jesus placed on the altar in heaven.

When the Bible compares the first Adam's sin to the necessity for a crucifixion, resurrection, and sacrifice on the altar, we must ask ourselves this question. Did Jesus shed His blood and sacrifice His life for an ancient allegorical story? Of course not! Otherwise, our faith would be futile.

And if Christ is not risen, your faith is futile; you are still in your sins!

1 Corinthians 15:17

The Mystery of Cain's Wife

Because Cain murdered his brother Abel, a mark was placed upon him, so he went to the city of Nod and took a wife (Genesis 4:16-17). Theologians have pondered this question for centuries: If the only people living on earth were Adam, Eve, and their three sons, where did Cain's wife come from and how could there be a city when there were no other humans? As a pastor, many have asked me this same question because they feel they have found a paradox or a glitch in the Bible. Every biblical question has an answer.

Let's ask ourselves, what do we know to be true? First, we know that Adam and Eve did not have any children before Eve was tempted and Adam sinned. How do we know that? If children had been born before the sin of Adam, those children would not have inherited Adam's sin nature. And we know that all mankind is born with Adam's sin nature (Romans 5:12).

Next, we know that no children were born in the Garden. How do we know that? Adam and Eve were driven from the Garden immediately after their sin.

Also, we know that all living humans are descendants of Adam and Eve. How do we know that? The Bible says that Adam was the first man (1 Corinthians 15:45) and Eve was the mother of all humanity.

> *Adam named his wife Eve. He gave her this name because Eve would be the mother of everyone who ever lived.*
>
> GENESIS 3:20 ERV

When Cain killed Abel, they were adults who had evidently lived long enough to have developed skills and trades. Cain farmed the land and grew crops; Abel raised sheep (Genesis 4:2). To understand farming and the care of animals must have come through trial and error and taken extended time as there was no previous generation to train them, other than Adam.

The Bible says Adam and Eve had many other children (Genesis 5:4), and apparently enough children that communities and cities were formed. The Bible does not say how long it was before Cain killed Abel, but obviously enough time had passed for a community to grow into a city named Nod.

Likewise, it's obvious that because Cain was a murderer and was marked as such, he was fearful for his own life (Genesis 4:14-15). There must have been enough people living at this time that a mark was necessary so that Cain would be recognized as a murderer. If the community of humans was small enough that everyone knew everyone else, a mark would not have been necessary.

After the murder, he fled to the city of Nod and took a wife who had to be a daughter, granddaughter, great-granddaughter, etc. of Adam and Eve.

By today's standards, that would be considered incest and against biblical law. But keep in mind that in these first generations of humans, the genetics were not imperfect as they are today and intermarriage was the only option for these first generations. It should be noted that this was also thousands of years before the law was given to Moses concerning intermarriage (Leviticus 18:6-18).

Sherlock Holmes was a detective in the mystery novels written by Sir Arthur Conan Doyle. Sherlock Holmes is famous for this statement: "When you have eliminated the impossible, whatever remains, however improbable, must be the truth."

With all of the impossibilities eliminated, we come to this truth. Cain's wife was a descendent of Adam and Eve. She lived in the city of Nod where Cain traveled and took her as his wife.

Chapter Three

THE WORLD BEFORE ADAM AND EVE

Before we dig deep into the subject of the world before Adam and Eve, I want to again make one thing perfectly clear. Neither belief nor unbelief about the pre-Adamic civilization affects your salvation. Your eternal life is not determined by your view of creation, but rather is simply determined by your belief in Jesus Christ as your Lord and Savior. Your belief about creation is *not* salvation critical. Do not allow your view of creation to separate you from your brothers and sisters in the body of Christ and keep you from walking in love.

A Scientific View of Creation

Scientists believe the universe was created out of a singularity smaller than an atom. In a moment of time shorter than a nanosecond, something unique happened. An unexplained explosion took place, and the universe came into existence. By measuring the radiation left over from this explosion, a picture can be recorded of the oldest light in the universe. This is basically how the age of the universe is determined.

Simply put, the leading scientific explanation of how our universe began is there was a spark, an explosion, and everything started expanding faster than the speed of light.

At this writing, the known universe is 94 billion light years across. This means that light traveling at 299,792,458 meters per second (or 186,282 miles per second) would take 94 billion years to travel from one side of the known universe to the other side of the known universe. And that is just as far as we can see.

With each new development in telescopes, we can see farther, and we discover billions more galaxies containing billions of stars. All this has been discovered in just the past few decades.

Most scientific groups agree that the universe was created approximately 13.8 billion years ago. However, this theory concerning the time the universe was created has changed several times and will probably continue to change as more discoveries are made.

Man's First Clear View of the Universe

While there is evidence that the understanding of telescopes was known in the late 1500s, the first telescope was created in the Netherlands in 1608. Through the years the designs gradually improved; but in the early 1900s things began to rapidly change. The Mount Palomar Telescope in San Diego was a great achievement; but nothing in the past could compare with the advancement that took place in the year 1990.

On April 24, 1990, NASA launched the Hubble Telescope. The Hubble Telescope was the first telescope to be launched into outer space and circle the earth about 340 miles above the atmosphere, which gives it a much greater view than any other previous telescope. Without being affected by the dense atmosphere, the rotation, and the vibration of the earth, this telescope has revolutionized the field of astronomy.

This telescope was named after Edwin Hubble who was born in Marshfield, Missouri, in 1889.

> *Up until the early 20ᵗʰ century, our perception of the cosmos fell within the bounds of the Milky Way. Although astronomers speculated about the existence of other galaxies in our universe, they had no observable evidence of them. It wasn't until Edwin Hubble pointed the Hooker Telescope at the constellation Andromeda that our perspective shifted. ...Hubble's continued observations of Andromeda resulted in one of the most transformative discoveries in cosmology. ... By 1929, Hubble had completely reimagined our place in the universe; not only was it home to millions of other galaxies, but the universe itself was expanding as well. ...Hubble's observations provided the earliest insight into the origins of our universe.[1]*

In 2004, NASA began the construction of a new telescope called the James Webb Telescope. It would reach 100

---

1 Edwin Hubble, Astronomer, NASA.gov; https://science.nasa.gov/people/edwin-hubble/; accessed March 18, 2024.

times farther into space than the Hubble and, of course, would reveal worlds never before seen. This telescope was successfully launched on December 25, 2021, and functioned perfectly. In a short time, trillions of new stars and hundreds of thousands of new galaxies were discovered, and new theories were presented concerning the time and method of the creation of our universe.

The Webb Telescope confirmed the reality that there is no empty space. Observations of small sections of space that were previously seen as empty revealed billions of galaxies each containing billions of stars.

With the reality of dark matter, our current revelation of truth is this—God's creation goes far beyond what we can see. The more we see of the creation of the God who is infinite, the more we realize our finite minds are limited. As the technology of scientific instruments increases, so will our knowledge, but we will never be able to fully comprehend the mind of the Creator.

So, let's take a look at what the Bible says about the time period after the original creation and before Adam and Eve were placed in the Garden of Eden.

The Ancient Past

In the beginning God created the heavens and the earth. The earth was without form, and void; and darkness was on the face of the deep. And the Spirit of God was hovering over the face of the waters.

GENESIS 1:1-2

בְּרֵאשִׁית בָּרָא אֱלֹהִים אֵת הַשָּׁמַיִם וְאֵת הָאָרֶץ׃
וְהָאָרֶץ הָיְתָה תֹהוּ וָבֹהוּ וְחֹשֶׁךְ עַל־פְּנֵי תְהוֹם וְרוּחַ אֱלֹהִים מְרַחֶפֶת עַל־פְּנֵי הַמָּיִם׃

GENESIS 1:1-2 (HEBREW)

In review, we can clearly see in Genesis 1:1 that God created the heavens (plural) and the earth. They were created perfect without any flaws or defects. Everything that God creates, He creates good. Again, this is confirmed by the prophet Isaiah when he said in Isaiah 45:18 that the earth was not created in vain.

> *For thus says the LORD, who created the heavens, who is God, who formed the earth and made it, who has established it, **who did not create it in vain**, who formed it to be inhabited: "I am the LORD, and there is no other."*

ISAIAH 45:18

The phrase "did not create it in vain" is translated from the Hebrew word *tohu*. This could be more correctly translated: He did not create it a desolation, a waste, without form, or in chaos.

Again, it's interesting to note that Genesis 1:2 says that the earth was without form and void. The phrase "without form, and void" comes from two Hebrew words—*tohu* and *va bohu*.

The best way to describe the meaning of this phrase would be like this. A Jewish mother went into her child's bedroom and cleaned it thoroughly. She put everything where it was supposed to be but later came back and saw that it was a total mess. The mother would say, *"Tohu va bohu!"* In other words, it became without form and void; it became chaotic, but it wasn't that way originally.

If the earth was not formless and void but perfect in verse 1, but was formless and void in verse 2, then we need to discover what the Bible says about what happened between those two verses. The Bible is true and will always confirm itself.

Something catastrophic must have happened between these two verses and it probably happened over a great amount of time. How long was the earth perfect before it was formless and void?

The first creation that was perfect is the creation where Lucifer lived before his fall. The Bible says that he (Lucifer) was perfect on the day that he was created (Ezekiel 28:15). So, we can see that the earth and Lucifer were both perfect.

Lucifer was a cherub (angel) in the kingdom of God (Ezekiel 28:14). His being was full of musical instruments (Ezekiel 28:13) and obviously was involved with the worship of Almighty God. Creation and the angels existed in harmony in the magnificent heavens that God created.

However, iniquity (sin) was found within Lucifer as he gathered together one-third of the angels of heaven to rebel against God. His pride and his arrogant belief in his own power caused him to declare that he would put his throne on the sides of the north with God.

> *How you are fallen from heaven, O Lucifer, son of the morning! How you are cut down to the ground, you who weakened the nations! For you have said in*

your heart: "I will ascend into heaven, I will exalt my throne above the stars of God; I will also sit on the mount of the congregation on the farthest sides of the north."

Isaiah 14:12-13

He greatly underestimated the power of his Creator who cast him down to planet Earth where he had previously deceived the kingdoms there. Because of his corruption, chaos and destruction prevailed, and the earth became formless and void. The kingdoms on the earth were destroyed. Jesus referred to him being cast down in Luke 10:18:

And He said to them, "I saw Satan fall like lightning from heaven."

Some have misinterpreted the time of Revelation 12:7-9 to imply that Satan's removal from heaven will be in the future. When Jesus spoke of Satan falling from heaven, He was obviously referring to an ancient past event. Satan was cast out of heaven and will never be in heaven again to require a future removal.

The earth became submerged in water and was formless and void. All of the kingdoms, the creatures, and the earth were destroyed by water. This was the first flood—the Luciferian flood.

The Beginning of Time

Time was created. How do we know this? Because in the Bible we are told that God made promises before time began. If time had a beginning, that means it was created and everything that was created was created by the Word of God.

> *In hope of eternal life which God, who cannot lie, promised* **before time began.**
>
> TITUS 1:2

So, God existed in the ageless past before time itself. Within God's Hebrew name is this reality: God was and is and is to come (Revelation 1:8). It is literally impossible to chronicle God's past because there is no beginning in Him.

However, the earth and the heavens do have a beginning. According to the Bible, much happened in the heavens and on the earth over a great period of time before man was created and placed in the Garden of Eden.

Before the earth became formless and void and before Day 1 of creation, there was great beauty in heaven. God created the angels and the heavenly hosts. Among these created beings, He created Lucifer. He was the anointed cherub that covered (Ezekiel 28:12-14).

> *Son of man, take up a lamentation for the king of Tyre, and say to him, "Thus says the LORD GOD: 'You were the seal of perfection, full of wisdom and perfect in beauty.'"*
>
> EZEKIEL 28:12

Some scholars claim this passage refers only to the king of Tyre and not to Satan. However, many times the prophets of the Old Testament, including Elijah, Isaiah, Jeremiah, and

Ezekiel used symbolic terminology in their prophecies and would foretell future events and re-tell past events cloaked within a message pertaining to current events.

Likewise, a contemporary person could be used as an illustration of a person from the past or the future. The apostle John used this method of prophecy in his revelation of the apocalypse. We find this method of prophecy with Isaiah when he makes reference to the king of Tyre and Satan, blending past, present, and future.

Why would Ezekiel refer to the king of Tyre and compare Satan to him? Possibly because the city of Tyre received some of the strongest prophetic condemnations in the Bible (Amos 1:9; Joel 3:4-8). Tyre was known for building its wealth through the exploitation of its neighbors.

Many ancient writings refer to Tyre as a metropolis filled with unscrupulous merchants. It was also considered to be the center of sexual immorality and religious idolatry. For this reason, the prophet Ezekiel paralleled the history of Satan.

You were in Eden, the garden of God; every precious stone was your covering: the sardius, topaz, and diamond, beryl, onyx, and jasper, sapphire, turquoise, and emerald with gold. The workmanship of your timbrels and pipes was prepared for you on the day you were created.

You were the anointed cherub who covers; I established you; you were on the holy mountain of God; you walked back and forth in the midst of fiery stones.

You were perfect in your ways from the day you were
created, till iniquity was found in you.
EZEKIEL 28:13-15

Consider the following as proof this passage is referring
to Lucifer:

1. Lucifer was in Eden and the king of Tyre was
   not.
2. Lucifer's covering included jewels and gold.
3. Musical instruments were part of his being.
4. He was created fully mature—not birthed.
5. He was present with God on the holy
   mountain.
6. He walked in the midst of the fiery stones.
7. Lucifer was created perfect.

The earthly human king of Tyre fits none of these descriptions.

Before the Re-Creation and Man

What specifically caused the chaos that destroyed the original creation and caused the earth to be flooded with water (the
Luciferian flood)?

Sadly, iniquity was found in the anointed cherub, Lucifer,
and he rebelled and was cast down to the earth. The Bible tells
us much about the time between Lucifer's creation and when
he was cast down. During this time period, there were kings,
kingdoms, nations, and commerce.

It would have taken a great amount of time for the world to separate into regions where kingdoms developed leadership, and methods of commerce became established. Although the Bible does not tell us exactly how long this period of time was, it must have been extensive.

> **By the abundance of your trading** *you became filled with violence within, and you sinned; therefore I cast you as a profane thing out of the mountain of God; and I destroyed you, O covering cherub, from the midst of the fiery stones.*
>
> EZEKIEL 28:16

In the Hebrew language, the word *ground* used in Isaiah 14:12 is *'erets.* This word can also be translated *earth.* Jesus said He saw Satan fall from heaven to the earth at lightning speed (Luke 10:18).

> *How you are fallen from heaven, O Lucifer, son of the morning! How you are cut down to the* **ground***, you who weakened the nations!*
>
> ISAIAH 14:12

In Jeremiah 4, there is an inserted prophetic re-telling that further enlightens us to a historical truth. Verses 23-26 reveal that Satan was cast down to the earth that was created to be inhabited, and that the earth changed and became formless and void. There was no light. The mountains and the hills trembled and moved back and forth, and all this happened before there was man. Did you notice that? When Lucifer was cast to the earth, man did not exist, but there were cities that were broken down.

> *I beheld the earth, and indeed it was without form, and void; and the heavens, they had no light. I beheld the mountains, and indeed they trembled, and all the hills moved back and forth.*
>
> *I beheld, **and indeed there was no man**, and all the birds of the heavens had fled. I beheld, and indeed the fruitful land was a wilderness, and all its cities were broken down at the presence of the LORD, by His fierce anger.*
>
> JEREMIAH 4:23-26

Further in Ezekiel 28, the Lord said that He cast Lucifer out of heaven as a profane thing out of the mountain of God, and then makes this astonishing statement. "Your heart was lifted up because of your beauty; you corrupted your wisdom for the sake of your splendor; I cast you to the ground, I laid you **before kings**, that they might gaze at you" (Ezekiel 28:17).

Who Were the Kings?

Who was the abundance of "trading" with (Ezekiel 28:16)? If there were kings, there would be kingdoms and nations, boundaries, and commerce. There was definitely some type of trading that existed among these nations, and Lucifer was engaged with the commerce, because Ezekiel refers to Lucifer when he says, "You defiled your sanctuaries by the multitude of your iniquities, by the iniquity of your trading" (Ezekiel 28:18).

Does this mean that mankind was on the earth before Adam? Definitely not! The Bible clearly tells us that Adam was the first man (1 Corinthians 15:45). However, there was an existence of some type of intelligent creature on the earth that had developed kingdoms with rulers and commerce that Lucifer was deeply involved with. Obviously, he deceived and cheated them.

Were these civilizations comprised of physical beings or spiritual entities? Obviously, there was a physical aspect to them because they operated on the earth in the natural realm of physics that God had placed in operation on the earth. Is it possible that it could be a combination of angelic beings and a physical non-human creation? And if a non-human physical creation existed, is it possible that it (they) had a soul?

The origin of the kings and kingdoms that traded with Lucifer and populated the earth before Lucifer's fall is not addressed in the Bible. However, an answer to this is addressed in some non-canonized ancient writings that may or may not be totally accurate. Ancient Hebrew texts, many of which were found in the Dead Sea Scrolls, suggest that these beings were angelic, and we know from many biblical references that angels can take on human form.

What Was Lucifer's Sin?

When they were young, each of my grandchildren asked me this question. "If God created everything, why did He create the devil?" The answer, of course, is that God didn't create the devil. He created Lucifer, who was perfect on the day he was created, but when iniquity (sin) was found in him, God cast him out of heaven, and he became the devil.

> *You were the seal of perfection, full of wisdom and perfect in beauty...**on the day you were created**.*
>
> EZEKIEL 28:12-13

Everything God creates is perfect (James 1:17) and has a purpose as well as a destiny. God did not create Lucifer and the angels to be like Him. They had a purpose, but being created in the image of God was not it.

In the book of Hebrews, we find the Bible clearly tells us why angels were created. They were created and put into position to minister for those who will inherit salvation (Hebrews 1:14). That's what the Bible says. Their purpose was three-fold: first and foremost, to worship God; second, to be His messengers; and third, to minister for those who will inherit salvation.

Mankind was created in the image and likeness of God and Jesus gave His life for mankind. The body of Christ—the church—are the ones who inherit salvation. Lucifer never said he was going to be God, he didn't say he was going to replace God, he just said, "I will be like God." Somehow, through his cunning and deceit, he convinced one-third of the heavenly hosts to follow him, and they, along with him, were cast out of heaven to the earth.

> *For you have said in your heart...**"I will be like the Most High."***
>
> ISAIAH 14:13-14

God requires every creation to stay in the lane (designed purpose) for which it was created. Throughout Scripture we find this common thread of truth. God's plan is that everything would reproduce after its own kind. Because of his pride, Lucifer attempted to change lanes and be something he was not created to be. He attempted to ascend into heaven, sit on a throne, and be like God (Isaiah 14:13).

There is only one place in Scripture that speaks of anyone seated on the throne other than the Father and the Son. According to Ephesians 2:6, the church is seated with Jesus in heavenly places. It was not Lucifer's place. That was Lucifer's sin.

> *And raised us up together, and made us **sit together in the heavenly places in Christ Jesus.***
>
> EPHESIANS 2:6

What a slap in the face it must have been for Satan to see Adam who was created in the likeness and image of God. His hatred for mankind—the creation he wanted to be—is evident throughout Scripture. The creation he was created to minister for now became the creation he wanted to steal from, kill, and destroy (John 10:10).

One can only imagine the rage Lucifer felt when the Father resurrected Jesus and redeemed mankind. Jesus, having gained all authority, then awarded that authority to those who follow Him. He said, "I give you authority…over all the power of the enemy, and nothing shall by any means hurt you" (Luke 10:19).

The World That Then Existed

There are craters on earth that are many miles in diameter that were created by meteor strikes. It's interesting that when some of these meteors are discovered, they are actually quite small. So how could a small meteorite create such a large crater? It's not the size necessarily, but more importantly, it's the velocity of the object hitting the earth.

Remember, Jesus said He saw Satan fall from heaven like lightning (Luke 10:18). We also know that one-third of the angels of heaven were cast down with him. Could it be that this anointed cherub and the fallen angels being slammed to the earth at 299,792,458 meters per second could have created a shock to planet Earth that was so great that oceans were shifted out of their basins, volcanic eruptions happened around the globe, and prehistoric animals were instantly killed?

Could this be the blow that knocked earth off its true axis? Is this why there is a difference between true north and magnetic north?

When the oceans swept across the earth, could it be that is the flood referred to in 2 Peter 3:5-6 where it says, "the world that then existed perished, being flooded with water"? This first flood, the Luciferian flood, destroyed the earth completely—it was formless and void. The second flood, the flood of Noah, only destroyed living creatures and humans on earth; the earth itself was not destroyed. The waters of the first flood were divided by God. The waters of the second flood receded naturally over several months.

The First Flood—Luciferian

Let's take a look at the Word of God and see what it has to say about the world that then existed.

Peter was not only a disciple, but a very close friend of Jesus. For three years they traveled together and undoubtedly Peter was taught consistently the things of God. Peter wrote to the church in his second letter the following statement:

> *For this they willfully forget: that by the word of God the heavens were of old, and the earth standing out of water and in the water, by which **the world that then existed perished**, being flooded with water.*
>
> 2 Peter 3:5-6

The phrase "the world that then existed" refers to a previous existence on the earth. Remember, this was a time when the earth had civilizations divided into kingdoms and Lucifer was involved with the commerce and trading on the earth. We are not told how long these civilizations existed, but they were obviously developed and probably greatly advanced.

Lucifer and the other angels were in the plan of God for the ages. This creation had a purpose but Lucifer in his pride rebelled against God and was defeated. The earth perished even though it had been created perfect for the future habitation of mankind. The condition of the earth was now formless and void and there was great darkness. The dry land was now covered with water. This first flood left the earth without hope.

Only God could redeem and refurbish the land that was destroyed by Lucifer's rebellion. The love and grace of God is so powerful that even though His creation turned against Him, His Spirit hovered over the face of the waters and He Himself, the Light, stepped into the darkness. The darkness fled and God started the restoration of the earth and His plan.

The Second Flood—Noah

The flood that occurred during the life of Noah was a result of the sin and depravity of man and of angels. This resulted in rain falling on the earth, creating a flood and the destruction of all living flesh—except for Noah and his wife, his three sons and their wives. When the rain ceased, the waters subsided over a period of time.

> *...And God made a wind to pass over the earth, and the waters subsided. The fountains of the deep and the windows of heaven were also stopped, and the rain from heaven was restrained. And the waters receded continually from the earth. At the end of the hundred and fifty days the waters decreased.*
>
> Genesis 8:1-3

As a result of the flood of Noah, all living flesh on the earth was destroyed. That included the Nephilim—the giants who were the children of the sons of God (Watchers).

After the flood, Noah was commissioned to replenish the earth. It is as though God hit the reset button and the development of the human race began again.

What Does the Bible Say?

As shown in this chapter, the Bible clearly describes a world that existed before the earth was covered with water. Kings ruled over kingdoms and Lucifer was involved with commerce. Lucifer led a rebellion and was followed by one-third of the angels. In his defeat, they were cast to the earth and the earth was destroyed by water.

The Bible clearly tells us that there were two distinctly different times that the earth was covered with water. The first time was after the perfect world became chaos because of the angelic sin of Lucifer. The second time was after the sons of God (Watchers) brought perversion into the earth that resulted in the altered genetics of the giants.

An understanding of the original creation and re-creation will clarify many questions and bring a deeper understanding of the Bible.

Chapter Four

The Watchers and the Nephilim

The book of Genesis records a historical event that is very misunderstood and ignored by much of the church clergy, because it is so bizarre and hard to comprehend. This event, combined with the perversion of man, brought the flood in the days of Noah.

"Now it came to pass, when men began to multiply on the face of the earth, and daughters were born to them, that the **sons of God** saw the daughters of men, that they were beautiful; and they took wives for themselves of all whom they chose. ...There were giants on the earth in those days, and also afterward, when the sons of God came in to the daughters of men and they bore children to them. Those were the mighty men (giants) who were of old, men of renown" (Genesis 6:1-2,4).

Who were these "sons of God" who took earthly wives and bore children? All ancient writings agree that the sons of God are angels. This includes the Book of Enoch, the Genesis Apocryphon, the Damascus Document, the Book of Jubilees, the Testament of Reuben, Second Barak, Josephus, and the Septuagint (the Greek version of the Hebrew Bible that many of the apostles used). Even the books of Jude and Second Peter in the Bible agree. Every one of them interpret "the sons of God" as angels.

Proof in the Book of Job

There are some secular scholars who say that Job was a mythical figure and not an actual human, thus relegating the entire book of Job as fiction. However, the Bible tells us that Job was a real person.

The word of the Lord came to Ezekiel, and he stood up and spoke on behalf of the Lord: "'Even if these three men, Noah, Daniel, and Job, were in it, they would deliver only themselves by their righteousness,' says the LORD God" (Ezekiel 14:14). God is speaking and says, "these three men," so they are not fictional characters, but real people: "Noah, Daniel, and Job." This lets us know that Job was a real person, which further verifies that what happened in the book of Job was real, not fictional.

The book of Job came from the writing section of the Hebrew Bible, the Tenach, and it's the first of the poetic books in our Bible. Scholars generally agree that the book of Job was written somewhere between the 4th and 7th century BC and that may or may not be correct. However, there is one thing we do know. In the entire 42 chapters of Job, the Law (the 10 written commandments and the 603 oral commandments that were given to Moses on Mount Sinai) is not mentioned even once. The book of Job most likely pre-dates the Law, which was given approximately 3,500 years ago. So, the following events in the book of Job are ancient events:

> *To what were its foundations fastened? Or who laid its cornerstone, when the morning stars sang together, and all the **sons of God** shouted for joy?*
>
> JOB 38:6-7

This passage in Job tells us the sons of God (the angels) were present at creation. They existed before the earth; they existed before the Garden of Eden. Ezekiel 28:13 says they were created, but they were created eons of time before man. Psalm 8 tells us they were watching as God created man. One of the angels asked God, "Why are people so important to you? Why do you even think about them? Why do you care so much about humans? Why do you even notice them?" (Psalm 8:4 ERV). It's almost like the angel was asking, "Aren't I enough?" Mankind was created to worship God and to fellowship with God for all eternity.

Another passage in the Bible describes the Lord's interaction with the sons of God. Job 1:6 says, "Now there was a day when the **sons of God** came to present themselves before the LORD, and Satan also came among them."

Keep in mind that when Satan was in heaven, his name was Lucifer. He was called Lucifer in the Bible, but when he was cast out, he became the adversary. The word *satan* means adversary—the one who comes against. From that point on he was called Satan, or the devil, the great dragon, the serpent of old.

So the great dragon was cast out, that serpent of old, called the Devil and Satan, who deceives the whole world; he was cast to the earth, and his angels were cast out with him.

REVELATION 12:9

Evidently the angels had to present themselves in submission to the Lord. So when the sons of God went to present themselves before the Lord, Satan went with them. He had obviously already been cast out of heaven; otherwise, he would have been called Lucifer. Therefore, this presentation before the Lord did not take place in God's heaven.

The ancient book of Job clearly states that the sons of God are angels.

The Sethite View of the Sons of God

Historically, the oldest interpretation and view is that the sons of God were angels like we have discussed. Some of those angels had sexual relations with human women, which produced an offspring of giants called the Nephilim. This was the accepted teaching during the time of Jesus and in the first century. It was supported by such people as the historian Flavius Josephus, and Eusebius (one of the early church leaders). It's also interesting that Justin Martyr, Origen, Irenaeus, and Clement of Alexandria, who were highly esteemed authors of their day, also held to the belief that the sons of God were angels.

All the apostles and the writers at the time of the apostles taught that "sons of God" were angels. It wasn't until centuries after Jesus that a new view was brought into existence. This is known as the Sethite view. This position says the sons of God were simply male offspring from the lineage of Seth. The wives they took (daughters of men) were simply women descendants of Cain. (Seth and Cain were sons of Adam and Eve.)

The first instance of this view can be traced to a Greek philosopher named Celsus. He stated that the sons of Seth were righteous and the daughters of Cain were evil. However, if you trace the genealogy in the Bible, you will find righteousness and unrighteousness in both family trees.

Early church leaders (Augustus of Hippo and Origen), as well as letters that were attributed to Clement, easily disproved the Sethite view simply by a basic scholarly review.

The Sethite view means that for some unexplainable reason, the human sons of Seth and the human daughters of Cain produced children with defective DNA that were the Nephilim (giants). This defies logic and would be genetically impossible.

It is apparent that the sons of God were angelic beings who descended on Mount Hermon and made a determined and willful decision to bear children by these earthly women. While it may be difficult to understand the physical union of an angel and a human and even more difficult to explain how this could happen, we must not ignore what the Bible says: The sons of God took wives and bore children. And all the scriptural references to the sons of God clearly show they were angels (Job 1:6, Job 2:1, and Job 38:7).

New Testament Sons of God Are Different

Keep in mind that the Old Testament is a Hebrew text, and the New Testament is basically a Greek text. The New Testament rendering of *sons of God* compared to the Old Testament rendering does not correlate. The New Testament rendering of *sons of God* is *teknon Theos* and ascribes what born-again believers become as well as their status in the kingdom to come. These should not be confused with the angelic term of the Old Testament. The sons of God of the Old Testament (angels) are to minister for the sons of God (born-again believers) of the New Testament (Hebrews 1:14).

> *For you are all sons of God through faith in Christ Jesus.*
>
> GALATIANS 3:26

> *Behold, what manner of love the Father hath bestowed upon us, that we should be called the sons of God....*
>
> 1 JOHN 3:1 KING JAMES VERSION

Simply put, the reference to the sons of God in the Old Testament are angels and reference to the sons of God in the New Testament are born-again believers who are a part of the body of Christ, the church.

Angels Who Sinned

There are two groups of angels who sinned. The first group are the angels who followed Lucifer in his rebellion before the creation of man. They were cast to the earth and have already been judged. The Bible tells us that hell was created specifically for the purpose of containing Satan and his angels for all eternity (Matthew 25:41). God has judged them, sentenced them, and determined their punishment.

Obviously, these are not the angels that will be judged by the church (1 Corinthians 6:3). How do we know this? Because the angels who fell with Lucifer have already been judged. The method and time of their execution has already been determined by God. So if the fallen angels are truly incarcerated on earth, why do they cause so much havoc in the lives of mankind?

A comparison could be a convicted murderer is placed in an area called death row in the prison. He has been sentenced to death by the judge, but there is time between sentencing and the execution of his punishment.

The angels that fell with Lucifer are now confined to earth and the church has been given full authority over them. We could say the church is the guard in the prison, so if we fail to use our authority, the prisoners have free rein of the prison.

> *I promise you God in heaven will allow whatever you allow on earth, but God will not allow anything you don't allow.*
>
> MATTHEW 18:18 CEV

Once again, their judgment has been pronounced and is recorded in the Bible. The method of execution has been determined and at the designated time will be carried out. Mankind gave up their authority over the devil when Adam sinned, but Jesus regained that authority for born-again believers.

The angels who continued in their God-ordained purpose (proper domain) and who stayed faithful under the leadership of God (Gabriel, Michael, etc.) will have no need of judgment. They have committed no sin.

The second group of angels who sinned are the 200 "Watchers" that were assigned to watch over humanity before Noah's flood. These are the sons of God of Genesis 6 who left their proper domain, descended on Mount Hermon, and made a pact to take earthly women as their wives and commit fornication (Genesis 6:1-2; Enoch chapter 7). These angels have been imprisoned in chains in Tartarus and reserved for judgment. Obviously, these fallen angels (sons of God) have not yet been judged and are most likely the angels that the Bible says the church will judge.

> *For if God did not spare the angels who sinned, but cast them down to hell and delivered them into chains of darkness, to be **reserved for judgment**; and did not spare the ancient world, but saved Noah, one of eight people, a preacher of righteousness, bringing in the flood on the world of the ungodly.*
>
> 2 Peter 2:4-5

> *Do you not know that we shall judge angels?*
>
> 1 Corinthians 6:3

During the early days of mankind outside the Garden, this group of angels was referred to as *ben elohim* or the sons of God. Their offspring was the Nephilim, which in Hebrew simply means fallen ones. They were the giants of ancient times.

The Overseers of Humanity

Watchers are angels who are assigned to watch over humanity.

Even though 200 of the watchers who were assigned to watch over humanity sinned, we must not forget there was an innumerable number of other angels who remained loyal to God. The archangel Michael and countless other angels retained their proper place in God's kingdom and continue to this day to protect, deliver, and be subject to the word of the King of the kingdom of God. Scripturally we know that watchers continued, and the book of Daniel refers to them:

> *And inasmuch as the king saw a watcher, a holy one, coming down from heaven and saying...*
> DANIEL 4:23

Who Were the Watchers Who Sinned?

In the Book of Enoch, the Watchers were specific angels dispatched to earth with the task of watching over mankind. However, under the leadership of the angel Semyaza, they left their assigned duty of watching over mankind and began to lust after earthly women. After taking earthly wives, they had children who were called Nephilim (giants). This led to the judgment of God, which brought the flood. Chapters 1-36 in the Book of Enoch are dedicated to the subject of the Watchers.

In the Book of Enoch, chapter 6, verses 5 and 6, it says, "So all together they bound themselves by an oath. There were **two hundred**, total, that descended in the days of Jared upon

Ardis, the summit of Mount Hermon. They called it Mount Hermon because they had sworn and bound themselves by oath upon it."[1]

Can Angels Have Children?

An extremely strong controversial subject among theologians is this question: Can angels procreate and have children? There has been great debate about whether the angels that sinned in chapter 6 of Genesis actually had sexual relations with earthly women or not.

Many would say that is impossible, but we need to look at what the Bible shows us. Yes, we know that angels can take on many forms and one of them is to appear human. For example, the two angels who spoke to the disciples at the ascension of Jesus had the appearance of men (Acts 1:10-11). Also, Abraham gave hospitality to the men who approached him without realizing that they were angels until later (Genesis 18).

The very fact that the Bible says they took them as wives and bore children to them would indicate an intimate relationship. In fact, some versions of the Bible even translate this verse as "the sons of God had intercourse with the daughters of human beings" (Genesis 6:4 New American Bible Revised Edition). The Bible tells us that the offspring born to them were the Nephilim (Genesis 6:4 ESV). These were the giants of old.

There are many thoughts regarding this, but we must remember that the Bible is true and contains truth. We may

---

1   Ken Johnson, Th.D., *Ancient Book of Enoch* (CreateSpace, 2012), 18.

wonder "how," but regardless of how, the Bible truth remains—they did, and the result was children (Nephilim) who were born as giants, the mighty men of renown.

History of the Book of Enoch

To get a more complete understanding of what happened, we can look at the Book of Enoch and see that the same event is recorded with more detail. While the Book of Enoch is not considered Holy Scripture, it brings understanding to the event.

If the legends are to be believed, Enoch passed his book and other books to Noah, who preserved them in the Ark. Noah then passed Enoch's book on to Shem, who preserved it in the city of Salem. Eventually it was passed down to the Israeli tribe of Levi for safekeeping. Somewhere along the line a new Hebrew translation renamed some of the place names of the cities, rivers, and lands. This was most likely done around the time of Solomon. It was then preserved up to the time the Essenes buried it, along with other ancient texts, to be found among the Dead Sea Scrolls.[2]

Interestingly, the Book of Enoch is a non-canonized pseudepigraphal book. The text is estimated to have been written in 300–200 BC, and the latter part (Book of Parables) most likely around 100 BC. No Hebrew version has survived, but some fragments written in Aramaic as well as Koine

---

2   Ken Johnson, *Ancient Book of Enoch*, 6.

Greek and Latin have been found in the Dead Sea Scrolls. This makes it evident that the Book of Enoch was known by Jews and early Christians. Several authors of the first century quoted the Book of Enoch. Jude, the half-brother of Jesus, quoted Enoch in his letter (Jude 1:14-15). Today the Book of Enoch only survives in its entirety in Ge'ez, an ancient South Semitic language.

The Book of Enoch is part of the biblical canon used by the Ethiopian Jewish community *Beta Israel*. It is also in the canonized version of the Christian Ethiopian Orthodox Tewahedo Church. Most Jewish and Christian groups accept Enoch as having some historical and theological content, but do not regard it as an official part of the canonized Scripture.

With this in mind, we will cautiously quote passages from the Book of Enoch referring to the sons of God. The Book of Enoch definitely says they are angels, even listing their names and explaining extensively both their motives and purposes.

Insight into the 200 Watchers

Enoch chapter six, verses one and two says, "It came to pass in those days that the children of men multiplied, and beautiful and fair daughters were born unto them. The angels, the sons of the heaven, saw and lusted after them, and said to one another, 'Come, let us choose wives from among the children of men and beget children.'"[3]

---

3   Ken Johnson, *Ancient Book of Enoch*, 18.

The Book of Enoch gives us more insight into these 200 Watchers who sinned. They did not just get tempted and fall into sin, but they deliberately chose to take earthly women as wives, fully knowing that there could be severe consequences for their actions. Enoch chapter six, verses three through five says, "And their leader, Semyaza, said to them, 'I am afraid that you will not truly agree to do this deed, and I alone will have to pay the penalty of this great sin.' They all answered him saying, 'We should all swear to bind ourselves by a mutual oath not to abandon this plan, but to do this thing.' So, all together they bound themselves by an oath."[4]

Enoch chapter six, verses seven and eight continues, "These are the names of their leaders: Semyaza, their leader, Arakibal, Rameel, Akibeel, Tamiel, Ramuel, Daniel, Ezeqeel, Barakel, Asael, Armaros, Batraal, Ananel, Zavebe, Samsapeel, Satarel, Turel, Yomyael, Sariel. These leaders led the rest of the two hundred angels."[5]

Enoch chapter seven, verses one and two describes what happened after they took the oath. "Each of the two hundred chose a wife for himself and they began to go in unto them and to mate with them, and they taught them sorcery and enchantments, and the cutting of roots, and made them acquainted with plants. These women became pregnant and gave birth to great giants, whose height reached up to three thousand ells."[6]

---

4   Ibid.
5   Ibid., 18-19.
6   Ibid., 19.

One might ask if the details in the Book of Enoch are true, then why are they not recorded in the writings of Moses in the book of Genesis? To answer this, we must understand that just because something is not in the Bible does not make it true or false. Every external writing must be examined in light of Scripture. Also, the Bible only reveals what is necessary. If every truth were written, the world would not be able to hold all the volumes (John 21:25). The account in Enoch concerning the sons of God (the Watchers who sinned) fits seamlessly with the account in Genesis.

Giant Perversion on the Earth

The giants (Nephilim) were so large that they consumed the earth's produce faster than it could grow. Apparently, humanity on earth attempted to supply enough food to keep the giants satisfied. However, their consumption was so great that it bypassed the ability of man to supply it. Food became so scarce for the giants that they resorted to consumption of human flesh and even cannibalism. The end result, if this were allowed to continue, would have been the total destruction of mankind.

The Book of Enoch in chapter seven, verses three and four, reveals the details of this savage destruction. "These giants consumed all the food; and when men could no longer sustain them, the giants turned against them and devoured mankind."[7]

---

7   Ken Johnson, *Ancient Book of Enoch*.

There were many other perversions also taking place on earth during this time. We find from the Book of Enoch and other ancient writings that some of this perversion had to do with the making of hybrids. Some of the offspring of the angelic/human/animal relationship was even part man/ part animal.

Enoch chapter seven, verses five and six gives details of this. "They also began to sin against birds, and beasts, and reptiles, and fish, and to devour one another's flesh, and drink the blood. Then the earth laid accusation against the lawless ones."[8]

> *You shall keep my statutes. You shall not let your cattle breed with a different kind....*
>
> LEVITICUS 19:19 ESV

Many ancient sculptures found in pyramids, temples, and tombs depict beings with the head of a bird and the body of a beast or a man. Could it be that the artist created something that he saw?

Could it be that the mythological stories about the ancient Greek gods were actually rooted in a truth that happened at the time before the flood of Noah? Could they have been the hybrid beings that many of the early civilizations of man called "gods"? Could it be that the ancient Greek and Roman gods of mythology actually had their roots in the reality of these fallen ones called the Nephilim?

---

8   Ibid.

Contaminating the DNA
of Mankind

What was the result of this incursion of angels into the repro-duction plan of God for man? While the Watchers were simply consumed by the beauty of the women and lusted after them, it resulted in the distortion of human DNA. Satan, who pos-sibly stood silently by while this was happening, could have seen it as an opportunity to destroy the seed of man. Could it be that once the sin was committed, Satan sought to amplify the perversion and ultimately pervert the Seed (Jesus) from being the perfect sacrifice? Obviously, Satan would not pass up this opportunity.

> *And I will put enmity between you and the woman, and between your seed and her Seed; He shall bruise your head, and you shall bruise His heel.*
>
> Genesis 3:15

If the seed that contains the genetic code (DNA) of man became contaminated, then there could not be a perfect sac-rifice. Because any sacrifice to God had to be perfect, Satan saw this contamination caused by the sin of the Watchers as an opportunity to pollute the entire lineage of man on earth, thus preventing the Seed of the woman from bringing about his destruction.

> *...For by the power of the eternal Spirit, Christ offered himself to God as a perfect sacrifice for our sins.*
>
> Hebrews 9:14 NLT

The Nephilim seed carried within it contaminated, distorted, and imperfect DNA. Within the sperm and the egg are the hands and feet, glands, organs, brain, nervous system, and every detail of the offspring. DNA makes man what he is, and the contamination caused the offspring to be giants—distorted man. In the same way a virus can spread through a civilization, so could the perverted genetics that resulted in the giants. Over time, all of mankind would become infected.

By contaminating the DNA of all mankind, there would be no one left who was not contaminated and that would prevent the birth of the perfect sacrificial Lamb of God. Because the blood and body of the Lamb had to be without spot or blemish, Satan thought he could prevent his own destruction that was prophesied in the Garden of Eden.

> *You shall not sacrifice to the LORD your God a bull or sheep which has any blemish or defect, for that is an abomination to the LORD your God.*
>
> DEUTERONOMY 17:1

Once the infection got into the genetic code, every descendant would be affected. But God found a man who was righteous, and his name was Noah. Noah was morally and genetically clean (no hybrid DNA) through all his generations before him. The genetic infection had to be stopped. Eliminated. Wiped out. That was one of the reasons for Noah's flood.

With the flood, all hybrid DNA was eliminated from the earth and only Noah, his wife, his three sons, and their wives remained for the repopulation of the earth.

Punishment of the Watchers

The punishment of the Watchers was different than the punishment of the angels who rebelled and fell with Lucifer. Because the Watchers did not keep their proper domain, and because their sin was so perverted and heinous, they were imprisoned in Tartarus (an area below Hades) until the great day of judgment.

> *And the angels who did not keep their proper domain, but left their own abode, He has reserved in everlasting chains under darkness for the judgment of the great day.*
>
> JUDE 1:6

Second Peter 2:4-5 says, "...**God did not spare the angels who sinned**, but cast them down to hell and delivered them into chains of darkness, to be reserved for judgment; and did not spare the ancient world, but saved Noah, one of eight people, a preacher of righteousness, bringing in the flood on the world of the ungodly."

Because these angels left their assigned duty, they were cast down into hell. The word *hell* there in the Greek text is *tartarus*. This is the only place in the Bible this word is used. The concept comes from Homer's epic writings, *The Iliad* and *The Odyssey*. The deepest part of Hades was Tartarus. Tartarus is defined as a place of torment as far below the earth as heaven is above the earth. These angels didn't just get confined to a regular prison, but to maximum security, and they were committed to chains in pits of darkness reserved for judgment.

According to the Bible, the final judgment will take place at the end of the millennium. From that point on, there will be no more death and all evil will be banished from earth and heaven. This is most likely when the judgment of the Watchers will take place and the church will most likely be the judge.

Why Did God Bring on the Flood?

Many years ago, I heard a person in a Sunday School class comment: "God is good, and He is evil, because after all, He brought the flood that killed everybody on the earth. Men, women, children. Killed them all."

However before the flood, perversion, debauchery, and even cannibalism were overtaking everything. These things were so prevalent that God had to intervene in order to save mankind from extinction. By saving the few remaining righteous in the ark, the flood put an end to the perversion and the evil that had permeated all society on the earth.

> *And behold, I Myself am bringing floodwaters on the earth, to destroy from under heaven all flesh in which is the breath of life; everything that is on the earth shall die.*
>
> GENESIS 6:17

God was not evil by bringing the flood to destroy all living things. It was actually an act of love, because if He had not intervened in the way He did, all of mankind would eventually have been contaminated, a Savior to redeem man could not have come, and all of mankind would have been hopelessly condemned to live in that depravity with no hope, no escape—essentially a life of hell on earth.

But the loving God, by destroying living things in the flood and preserving a remnant of mankind and animals, was able to essentially start over with His original goal of restoring humans to fellowship with Him for all eternity. By washing the earth with the flood, He cleared the way for the Messiah to give His life as the ultimate sacrifice.

In Old Testament times, the priests were not allowed to sacrifice a lamb that had a flaw. It had to be without spot or blemish. That was God's law. In order for the perfect sacrifice, the Lamb of God, to be placed on the perfect altar in heaven, the sacrifice had to be without spot or blemish.

God took everything that was not perverted and put it on the ark with Noah and his family. Everything not on the ark perished in the flood. Could this be why some ancient species are extinct?

God Had a Plan

God had a plan for the redemption of mankind. First Peter 1:20 says, "He indeed was foreordained before the foundation of the world, but was manifest in these last times for you."

God can do something that the devil can't do, and that we can't do, and no other being in existence can do except Him: He is omnipresent both in location and in time. He can see as far back into the past or as far into the future as

He wants. He can observe what is going to happen before it happens. He speaks it to His prophets by the Holy Spirit then they speak it.

The devil doesn't know the future. He still thinks he can win. Satan has lied so much that he believes his own lies and somehow thinks he can stop the progress of God's prophecies from coming to pass.

Interesting Genealogy

There are several ancient non-biblical writings that have survived through the centuries that give a more detailed account of Noah's family. One such account is found in the Book of Jubilees, which is canonized by the Ethiopian Orthodox Church. It lists the names of the wives of the men on the ark. Emzara is Noah's wife. Shem's wife is Sedeqetelebab; Ham's wife is Na'eltama'uk; Japheth's wife is Adataneses.

The Book of Jubilees also tells us that each son built a city, naming them after their wives. While this information may seem irrelevant and varies slightly in details from other manuscripts, all of them agree on the reality of the flood of Noah and his prodigy repopulating the earth.

Noah's descendant, Abram (Abraham), was born only 292 years after the flood. Noah lived until the age of 950 and was 600 years old at the time of the flood, which means he lived 58 years after Abram was born. However, it is unlikely that Abram and Noah actually met, because Abram was not called by God until he was 75 years old.

Abraham's son was Isaac, his grandson was Jacob, and one of Jacob's sons was Levi. The Testament of Levi was found in the Dead Sea Scrolls containing much family history. In fact, Shem (the son of Noah) lived past the flood longer than any of the other human occupants of the ark. Abraham, a descendant of Shem, was born 392 years after Shem. We know that Abraham lived to the age of 175 (Genesis 25:7), which means Shem outlived Abraham by 32 years.

After the call of Abraham, Shem was the only living person on earth who was alive before the flood of Noah and witnessed the Nephilim and all the perversion on the earth which prompted the cleansing of the earth by water. Shem was 100 years old at the flood and lived 500 more years after the flood (Genesis 11:10-11). We know Abraham had a relationship with Shem, as Shem sat in the office of Melchizedek and Abraham gave him a tithe of all.

The Return of the Giants

Genesis 6:4 says, "There were giants on the earth in those days, **and also afterward….**"

It is a reality that there were tribes of Nephilim (giants) on the earth after the flood. But how could this be true if they were all killed in the flood?

God called Abram out of Ur 422 years after the flood. His grandson's name was Jacob, whose name was changed to Israel. Jacob's (Israel's) twelve sons became the twelve tribes of Israel. Through a series of events and the passage of time, the

Hebrews lived in the land of Goshen under the rule of Egypt. Moses became their leader and took them on a 40-year journey to the Promised Land where they encountered giants.

In 1445 BC, Moses sent the twelve spies into the Promised Land who came back with this report: "We even saw the Nephilim there—the descendants of Anak come from the Nephilim! To ourselves we seemed like grasshoppers, and we must have seemed the same to them" (Numbers 13:33 Holman Christian Standard Bible).

When the Israelites left Egypt, they encountered many giants including Rapha'im, Horim, Avim, and the Anakim. The Anakim were possibly the most feared because Moses wrote in Deuteronomy 9:2 (New American Standard Bible), "Who can stand against the sons of Anak?"

The Israelites had experienced many miracles of deliverance. They experienced the dividing of the Red Sea, which allowed their escape from and the destruction of the Egyptian army. But even though God miraculously delivered and protected them over and over again, they still feared the Anakim.

The Anakim were not just tall men but were descendants of the Nephilim, which indicates they were genetically different. Amos 2:9, in describing the giants, says they were as tall as the cedars and as strong as the oaks.

King Og, the king of Bashan, was one of the last remaining giants of his tribe. He slept on a bed that was more than 13 feet long and 6 feet wide, and he filled the bed (Deuteronomy 3:11 NLT). He was killed by Moses (Deuteronomy 1:4).

Other Giants After the Flood

The Israelites were originally told to wipe out the Anakites, the Nephilim, and other giant tribes. In their conquest of the Promised Land, they were told to eliminate them completely. However, they didn't do it. One tribe survived and settled in the land of Gath and its surrounding cities. Their descendants were known as the Philistines.

Before David was king and just a teenager, he delivered Israel by killing the giant, Goliath, with a slingshot. The Bible says that Goliath had brothers (1 Chronicles 10:5; 2 Samuel 21:15-22) who were descendants of the Nephilim. It's interesting that in a war in Gath (Gaza), one giant had six fingers on each hand and six toes on each foot. When he defied Israel, Jonathan (King David's nephew) killed him (2 Samuel 21:20-21).

Flavius Josephus was born in Jerusalem and recorded Jewish history. In his historical writings concerning the giants, he stated:

> *For which reason they removed their camp to Hebron; and when they had taken it, they slew all the inhabitants. There were till then left the race of the giants, who had bodies so large and countenances so entirely different from other men, that they were surprising to the sight, and terrible to the hearing. The bones of these men are still shown to this very day, unlike to any credible relations of other men....[9]*

---

[9] *The Words of Flavius Josephus*, Book V: Chapter II: The Antiquities of the Jews 3.

The following list is from the Jewish Encyclopedia and refers to seven tribes of giants that are found in the Hebrew Bible:

1. Nephilim = (napal) violent or fallen ones, because they cause the world to fall and fill themselves

2. Rapha'im = (dead) because their sight makes people fearful and melt like wax; example Goliath of Gath and his brothers

3. Anakim = (sons of Anak) because they wore huge necklaces in great numbers

4. Zamzummin = because they were great warriors and inspired fear

5. Emim = because of their great size whoever saw one was seized with terror

6. Gibborim = because their brains (cranium) were large

7. Avim = because they destroyed the world and were themselves destroyed[10]

Among the North American Indians there are legends of giants with six fingers. One legend passed down through the generations is that upon greeting a stranger, the purpose of raising the right hand was to verify five fingers, and make sure the stranger had no association with the ancient vicious giants.

---

10   Dennis G. Lindsay, D.Min., *Giants, Fallen Angels and the Return of the Nephilim* (Shippensburg, PA: Destiny Image Publishers, 2018), 31.

Why Were There Giants After the Flood?

Keep in mind that Israel encountered the giants in the Promised Land approximately 1,300 years after the flood of Noah. If all of the Nephilim (giants) were killed in the flood, then how could Goliath be a descendant of the Nephilim? If all the giants before the flood were wiped out, how did the giants appear after the flood?

One ancient Jewish writer wrote that they hung on the side of the ark! That's an interesting thought, but it cannot be true because the Bible tells us all living beings perished in the flood except those on the ark.

There are several views as to how giants appeared on the earth for hundreds of years after the flood. Although the Bible does not give us a definitive answer of how the Nephilim (giants) reappeared after the flood, there are two prominent views.

1. The second incursion view: The same thing that happened before the flood happened after the flood. In other words, other sons of God once again committed fornication with earthly women and produced Nephilim.

2. The Ham's wife view: This view suggests that Ham's wife carried Nephilim DNA in her body on the ark. The lineage of the giant tribes can be traced back to Ham and his wife.

It's evident from many scriptures that there were several tribes of giants after the flood. In 1 Samuel 15:3, God commanded the Israelites to "go and attack Amalek, and utterly destroy all that they have, and do not spare them. But kill both man and woman, infant and nursing child, ox and sheep, camel and donkey."

Why would God issue a command of this severe nature? Quite simply, the defective Nephilim DNA in the giant tribes had to be eliminated. Before the flood, the contamination was so out of control that God Himself had to step in and complete the elimination of the Nephilim. After the flood, He gave this task of cleansing the land to the nation of Israel. They were to move into the Promised Land and eliminate all traces of the Nephilim. Eventually, Israel completed the work set before them, and the giants were wiped out.

What Does the Flood Have to Do with Us?

"God so loved the world that He gave His only begotten Son, that whoever believes in Him should not perish but have everlasting life. For God did not send His Son into the world to condemn the world, but that the world through Him might be saved. He who believes in Him is not condemned; but he who does not believe is condemned already, because he has not believed in the name of the only begotten Son of God" (John 3:16-18).

So why was there a flood? It was because He loves you! Why did He kill the giants? Because He loves you. He sacrificed His Son, His only begotten Son, because He loves you. And He wants us to receive this free (to us) gift that was very costly to Him.

Romans 10:9-10 tells us how to receive this free gift: "If you confess with your mouth the Lord Jesus and believe in your heart that God has raised Him from the dead, you will be saved. For with the heart one believes unto righteousness, and with the mouth confession is made unto salvation."

Do you believe that Jesus Christ was raised from the dead by His Father? Is Jesus Christ your Lord?

Summary

Sometimes the question is asked, "If God is a good God, and if He controls everything, then why does He allow evil to exist?"

The question itself is built on the assumption that God controls everything. While it is true that He controls all creation, you will discover by a basic reading of the Bible that He gives all sentient beings the gift of free choice.

Lucifer and his followers had the freedom to live in Paradise or to rebel. They chose poorly and were cast out. Adam was given the ability to live forever in the Garden God made for him, but he chose poorly and was cast out. The Watchers were sent to oversee mankind and have their abode in the heavens, but they chose poorly and were imprisoned.

Years ago, when my oldest granddaughter Karissa was young, she asked me this question. "Grandpa, what if the devil decides to get saved?"

That's an interesting question, but as far as we know from the Bible, there has never been a sacrifice made for the redemption of angels or any spirit being—other than mankind. They are judged by their own disobedience and separated eternally from God without there being any structure for a readmittance into His kingdom.

Mankind on the other hand, has a method of redemption available through the blood of Jesus, the perfect Sacrifice who was placed on the altar in heaven on the day of His resurrection.

In Him we have redemption through His blood, the forgiveness of sins, according to the riches of His grace.

EPHESIANS 1:7

The Sacrifice on the altar in heaven was for mankind—the descendants of Adam, not for angels. The fallen angels will always remain fallen.

For indeed He does not give aid to angels, but He does give aid to the seed of Abraham.

HEBREWS 2:16

And if you are Christ's, then you are Abraham's seed, and heirs according to the promise.

GALATIANS 3:29

But God, in His massive love, has always cleaned up the mess made by wrong decisions as the result of disobedience. Then He made a way for all people to be redeemed and to live as originally intended. God is love and His love endures forever.

Chapter 5

WHO BUILT
THE ANCIENT
STRUCTURES?

Around the world there are thousands of ancient structures that are built with such precision that modern man cannot explain how they were constructed without the aid of modern equipment. Many of these could not even be duplicated with the machinery that is available today.

Who built these ancient structures? How were they able to cut the stones (which many times were hard granite) with such razor-sharp precision that it defies comprehension of how it was achieved? Who built these ancient megalithic wonders and where did they attain the mathematic, scientific, cosmic information, knowledge, and skills required? How did they move the massive megalithic stones that many times came from quarries that were miles away?

First of all, we must understand that all the ancient structures discovered and examined by archeologists were not built in the same time period. Without understanding who was on the earth during the time of their construction, it would be difficult to determine who the builders were.

With that in mind, let's take a look at some of these mysterious structures.

Mysterious Structures

The island of Malta specifically played a vital strategic role in World War II as a base for the Allied Powers.

But centuries before that, it was home to the Knights Templar who built enormous fortresses and temples that stand to this day. These structures are visited by millions of tourists because of their massiveness and the secrets they contain.

But millennia before all of this, there were other ancient temples and structures that reveal a past that could only be inhabited by a civilization that had immense strength and access to beings with higher intellect and skills.

Many structures reveal an ancient past that challenges rational thinking about ancient history. One such structure is the Ħal Saflieni Hypogeum.

The Hypogeum

On one of my trips to Malta with two of my friends, L.A. Marzulli and Bob Ulrich, we explored the Hypogeum, which is now overseen by the United Nations Educational, Scientific and

Cultural Organization (UNESCO). Before we could enter the Hypogeum, they required us to put all communication devices, lights, cameras, etc. into a locker. Only one group of 10 people is allowed to enter at a time, and that usually requires a wait of several months. But because of one of my personal contacts in Malta, we were given special entry.

The word *hypogeum* simply means "underground" in Greek. The Hypogeum was accidentally discovered in 1902 while workers were cutting a cistern for a new housing development.

They started excavation in 1903 and discovered a large underground palace hewn from solid stone. The palace contained thousands of skeletons, some of which had elongated skulls. For some unknown reason, the contents (including artifacts found in graves with human remains) were emptied and discarded without being properly cataloged.

Excavations continued, and in 1908 visitors were allowed to observe the ongoing discoveries. It's estimated the Hpyogeum was in use at least 6,000 years ago. There is a lower main chamber that is called "The Holy of Holies." During the winter solstice, it is illuminated when light comes through its original opening above.

There is also a room called the "Oracle Room" that was studied in 2014 by an international team of scientists for the sole purpose of analyzing the acoustics. The rock was hewn in such a way that one man speaking in a normal voice from a certain place in the Oracle Room could speak to thousands throughout the Hypogeum and be easily heard. As Bob, L.A., and I stood in that place in the Oracle Room and spoke, we were amazed as our voices carried throughout the massive underground palace. Interesting fact: women's voices do not carry in the same way.

There are many other interesting details and numerous artifacts that were discovered in the Hypogeum, but to detail all of them would require more than a section in a book. However, I would like to recount a historical event concerning the Hypogeum that will give the true feeling of the massiveness of this underground ancient palace hewn from solid rock.

On the third and lowest level of the Hypogeum, in one of the burial chambers, is a doorway into another underground world. However, after the refurbishment of the Hypogeum, this lower level is no longer accessible to visitors. But why is this lower level and passageway no longer accessible?

The Lost Students

Many years ago, before the lower level was sealed, a teacher and her 30 students entered the underground palace for a field trip. At that time, it was reported that there were several overlapping layers of tunnels, and one could travel across the country—even under the Mediterranean Sea all the way to Rome. It was also reported that in the 16th century, the knights built fortifications over broken passageways and blocked doorways.

In the August 1940 issue of the *National Geographic* magazine, there is a story of students being lost in the massive network of tunnels. They were never found. The following is an excerpt from that magazine article:

> *While we cycled homeward, our friends told us that the island was honeycombed with a network of underground passages many of them catacombs.*
>
> *Years ago we could walk underground from one end of Malta to the other, but all entrances were closed by the Government because of a tragedy.*
>
> *On a sightseeing trip, comparable to a nature study tour in our own schools, a number of elementary school children and their teachers descended into the tunneled maze and did not return.*
>
> *For weeks, mothers declared that they had heard wailing and screaming from underground. But numerous excavations and searching parties brought no trace of the lost souls. After three weeks they were finally given up for dead.*[1]

Interesting Structures in Malta

As an eyewitness to the Hypogeum and the ancient temples of the giants on the islands of Malta and Gozo, I can testify that these ancient structures hold many secrets that the natural human cannot comprehend.

Who were these ancient people who numbered in the tens of thousands and lived completely underground in a series of

---

1 *National Geographic* magazine, Volume LXXVIII (Washington, DC: National Geographic Society, August 1940), 272.

hewn-from-stone tunnels and palaces? Where are the giants who occupied the temples that are scattered aboveground throughout the nation of Malta?

How do we explain the ancient "railway lines" carved into solid rock that stretch from one end of the island nation to the other? These railway lines are estimated to be at least 7,000 years old or possibly even older. If Adam left the Garden of Eden in 4004 BC as the Bible says, then how could a civilization be in existence a minimum of 1,000 years before the departure from Eden? Likewise, many artifacts discovered in Malta date back tens of thousands of years earlier.

If this time dating is correct, then the structure must have been constructed by the angels and non-humans before Adam left the Garden in 4004 BC. How do we explain the skeletons found? That can be easily answered by understanding that a future civilization could easily occupy a previously built structure. Structures built pre-Adam and pre-flood could obviously be occupied by post-flood humans. In other words, a civilization could build a structure and at a later time in history, when the structure has been abandoned, could be occupied by a later civilization. Structures of stone would not necessarily be destroyed by the waters of a flood.

Second Oldest Temple on the Planet—Ġgantija

Also, within Malta are some of the most interesting ancient archaeological discoveries. It has been called the land of the giants because many ancient temples and unexplained artifacts are plentiful there. Ggantija, the second-oldest temple and man-made structure found anywhere on the planet, is located in Malta. This megalithic complex is thought to have been erected as far back in time as 3600 BC. That would mean that it predates the flood of Noah's day by many centuries. By biblical chronology, Adam would have been about 400 years old at the time of the construction.

It is thought to be a place of ritual significance. Some of the stones used to build the complex are massive, measuring five meters (about 16 feet) in height and weighing as much as 50 tons. Archeologists and engineers have not been able to explain how an early agricultural society, equipped with only stone tools at its disposal, could have moved the massive megalithic stones.

While there, I asked one of the guides this question, and his reply was almost humorous. He pointed to a group of round stones about one foot in diameter that were scattered around the temple and around several of the other structures on the island. He claimed the huge megalithic stones were rolled on those small stone balls.

Given the long distance the stones were moved from where they were quarried, their massive weight, the rough uneven terrain, and the fact that the small round stones would have simply been crushed from the weight, the answer was obviously the politically correct, talking-point answer required to be given by the governing authority (UNESCO).

However, the residents have a legend passed through the generations that gives another explanation of the overwhelmingly impossible construction of the Ggantija Temple. The legend says that the temple was dedicated to a goddess named

Sansuna, who was a giantess that bore a child to one of the local men. The legend says that Sansuna was from the island of Gozo and was the builder of Ġgantija. She went to the town of Ta' Cenc, carried huge stones 4 kilometers (about 3 miles), then placed them at Ġgantija, "The Place of Giants." She did this in a single day by transporting the stones on her head while holding her half-giant, half-human baby over her other shoulder.

A second legend that seems more likely is that the structure served as a defensive tower, again built by a race of giants. But either way, the folklore involves giants of enormous size and strength.

As we approached the temple, an enormous wall of gray interlocking monoliths, some weighing at least 20 tons, rose into view. Without the modern equipment of today, the feat of constructing this temple complex would seem to be impossible.

Is it possible that the builders of this temple complex (assembled 5,500 years ago) had assistance from or even been completely built by giants? This timeframe was after Adam's sin and banishment from the Garden of Eden, and before the flood of Noah's day. And Genesis 6:4 says that during this time, "there were giants on the earth in those days, and also afterward."

Göbekli Tepe

Göbekli Tepe is a Neolithic site in southeastern Türkiye (formerly Turkey). The site is marked by layers of carved megaliths and is estimated to have been constructed in approximately 10,000 BC.

At Göbekli Tepe there are T-shaped limestone megaliths, some of which are more than 16 feet (five meters) high, weighing as much as 50 tons. The megaliths are arranged in circular formations positioned on top of one another. Some of the megaliths are carved with elaborate designs featuring foxes, lions, scorpions, and other images.

Although Göbekli Tepe predates Stonehenge by 6,000 years, it was not seriously investigated until the 1990s. Most experts identify it as a ritual site.

Because of the remains at the site, some archeologists believe that Göbekli Tepe was constructed by hunter-gatherers. But how did this hunting, agricultural pre-historic tribe move, carve, and strategically place the massive monoliths? Did they have help? Could that help have come from fallen angels? If this structure is estimated to have been in use 12,000 years ago, then we can calculate that time to be 6,000 years before Adam and Eve were driven out of the Garden of Eden.

Who were these inhabitants? According to the Bible, they could not have been human because Adam was the first human being, but they must have been humanlike. Or could they have been a civilization of fallen angels, a mixture, or a hybrid civilization?

The Sphinx of Giza

The Sphinx of Giza is one of the most mysterious construction projects in the world. It is over 60 feet in height, 240 feet in length, and hewn from one stone. Located on the Giza Plateau, 10 kilometers (6 miles) west of Cairo in Egypt, it is near the three great pyramids of Khufu, Khafre, and Menkaure. This structure is estimated to have been constructed sometime between 5000 BC to 8000 BC. If this dating is correct, this could be another structure that pre-dates Adam and was not built by man. Who could have built the sphinx?

The Pyramids of Egypt

The great pyramids of Egypt have baffled archeologists and the scientific community for centuries. There are currently more than 118 pyramids that have been discovered in Egypt. Archeologists believe there are more yet to be discovered.

Their construction defies logic. Modern engineers and geologists have been unable to determine how the ancient builders designed the foundations. Modern buildings settle at a rate of 6 inches per 100 years. There are great communities and cities that are literally sinking. In fact, the U.S. Capitol Building has settled over 5 inches since its construction in 1793. Yet the Great Pyramid has only settled one-half inch in over 5,000 years and the blocks used in its construction weigh approximately 6 million tons.

How did the ancients of Egypt understand geology and engineering to a greater degree than the modern engineers of today? The Great Pyramid is constructed with 2.25 million blocks. Each block was cut, transported, and then assembled with razor-like precision with only 2/100ths of an inch spacing between the stones.

Traditional teaching has been that the Great Pyramid was constructed in 20 years. This would mean that each stone had to be quarried, transported a great distance, cut to precision, and put into place in less than five minutes to fit that time frame, which of course seems impossible.

Archeologists are still discovering secrets hidden within the Great Pyramid. In 1940, a pilot for the British Air Force flying over the Great Pyramid of Giza discovered it had eight sides instead of four. At dawn and sunset during the spring and autumn equinox—when the sun casts a slight shadow— the eight sides can be clearly seen from the air. This required an extremely precise alignment of this 6-million-ton monument millennia ago. Did the ancients have greater knowledge of geology and science than we do today? Or were they assisted by more advanced beings?

Newgrange

Newgrange is located in the Boyne Valley of Ireland. It is a 5,200-year-old passage tomb that is said to have been built by the Stone Age farmers. The mound covers an area of one acre and is about 13 meters (about 43 feet) high and 85 meters (about 279 feet) in diameter.

A passage of 19 meters (about 62 feet) leads to a chamber with three alcoves. Newgrange is encircled by 97 engraved monoliths called kerbstones. Among them, the most fascinating is the one on the entrance containing symbols and hidden meanings.

Its estimated construction date is 3200 BC, and some archeologists believe it to be older than Stonehenge and the Giza Pyramids. The mound is enriched with megalithic art and is known as the jewel in the crown of Ireland's Ancient East.

Although it is called a "passage tomb," this is an understatement for this colossal house of astronomical significance. Why? The alignment within the chamber creates illumination with the rising sun in the winter solstice. The dramatic illumination of the passage and chambers during every winter solstice lasts for about 17 minutes. This makes Newgrange the most accurate time-telling device of that time.

Is it possible the inhabitants that archeologists believe were farmers could have had knowledge so advanced, and engineering skills so precise that they could have constructed Newgrange? Or is there another explanation? Who was living at that time who had the strength and the engineering skills to construct this ancient timepiece? Who understood the alignment of the stars?

It is believed by modern archeological theory and by conventional wisdom that the giant monoliths and monuments were built by local farmers for the purpose of social and religious reasons.

However, the monoliths, aligned with the celestial bodies' astronomic events, suggest that the builders were far advanced in their understanding of complex star-charts, astronomical theories, and engineering, which enabled them to produce boulders with mathematical precision. The question again arises. How could an agrarian society with stone and wood tools accomplish this? Did they have help? What do the ancient writings say about this?

The Book of Enoch tells us the Watchers taught men the knowledge of the planets, stars, and constellations. Enoch chapter eight, verse three says, "Semyaza taught enchantments, and root-cuttings. Armaros taught how to resolve enchantments. Barakel taught astrology. Kokabel taught the constellations (signs). Temel taught the knowledge of the clouds (astrology). Asradel taught the courses of the moon."[2]

So, could it be the ancient people got their knowledge of the cosmos from the 200 Watchers who mated with earthly women and produced the giants? Could it be this advanced knowledge and assistance from the Watchers and giants enabled them to move the massive intricately hewn stones? Could their advanced knowledge of the cosmos have guided and assisted the ancient beings and early humans with the precise solstice alignments? Neither the Bible nor the ancient writings contradict this possibility.

Remember what the Bible says about this time period (after Adam left the Garden but before the flood of Noah): "There were giants on the earth in those days, and also afterward..." (Genesis 6:4).

The Tower of Babel

As the waters subsided from the flood of Noah, God gave him and his sons (Shem, Ham, and Japheth) a command. He said, "Be fruitful, and multiply, and replenish the earth" (Genesis 9:1 American Standard Version). His three sons produced generations of descendants. But within a century or so, their descendants had not fulfilled the command to fill the earth.

---

2 Johnson, *Ancient Book of Enoch*, 20.

At the rate of procreation through the genealogy listed in the Bible, there could have been hundreds of thousands of descendants gathered together at Shinar.

Instead of fulfilling God's command, they settled in the land of Babylonia, and they all spoke one language. The Bible says they said to each other: "Come, let's build a great city for ourselves with a tower that reaches into the sky. This will make us famous and keep us from being scattered all over the world" (Genesis 11:4 NLT).

It's possible that because the flood was in the not-too-distant past, one of the purposes of the tower was to have a place above the flood line where they could feel they would be safe. They put their faith in themselves rather than God. God had proclaimed that the flood of Noah's day was the last flood and secured His promise with a covenant, represented by a rainbow.

But full of pride, these descendants of Noah decided to make a name for themselves and build a fortress where they could remain together. Because the builders of Babel all spoke one language, God said that nothing was impossible for them. He confused their language; and without communication with each other, construction stopped, and they were dispersed.

And the Lord said, Behold, they are one people and they have all one language; and this is only the beginning of what they will do, and now nothing they have imagined they can do will be impossible for them.
GENESIS 11:6 AMPLIFIED CLASSIC EDITION

This sounds very similar to the attempt Lucifer made after the original creation. Because Lucifer attempted to ascend into the heavens, he was cast to the earth. Likewise, the builders of the tower of Babel attempted to reach into the heavens, but instead were dispersed around the earth. In both cases, pride was their downfall.

Near 700 BC, Nebuchadnezzar built Babylon to its height of glory. It was the largest and wealthiest city in the world at that time. Under the rule of King Nebuchadnezzar, it grew to the size of a major city as large as Chicago. It had towering temples and beautiful palaces, with city walls wide enough for two chariots to ride side by side. It was also home to one of the seven wonders of the ancient world, the Hanging Gardens of Babylon.

The glory of Babylon was short-lived, however. After Nebuchadnezzar's death, Babylon was taken over by the Persian conqueror Cyrus II, who reduced the city to just an outpost of his kingdom.

In spite of the attempt to build a city and a tower after the flood, and in spite of all of the later attempts to build and maintain a large city, Babylon now is just rubble, 55 miles south of Baghdad. When God condemns a project, no man can successfully rebuild and maintain it.

There are archeological remains of the tower of Babel in Iraq, and the remains of Noah's ark have been discovered in the mountains of Ararat. Archeology can be interesting and the builders of ancient structures and artifacts, like the tower of Babel and Noah's ark, are clearly defined in Scripture.

Bible Timeline of Periods of Civilizations

Along with the monuments previously mentioned that are found in Malta, Türkiye, Iraq, Egypt, and Ireland, almost every country on earth has ancient structures too numerous to list. Some structures, such as Stonehenge and the Great Pyramid, are well known, but the number of ancient structures throughout the world is staggering. Although most are not specifically mentioned in the Bible, their existence is a reality. Is it even possible to learn who built these unexplainable structures?

In determining who the contractors and laborers of ancient structures were, we must ascertain the dates of their construction and look to the Bible to determine who was living on earth at the time of the construction. With that in mind, let's look at the following groupings.

1. Original Creation (Genesis 1:1) until the Luciferian Flood (Genesis 1:2)

This is the time period when there were civilizations on the earth of angels and possibly nonhuman beings that had developed kingdoms with trade and commerce. During this time is when Lucifer possibly ruled and later rebelled and was cast to the earth and confined along with all of the angels who followed him. After his fall to the earth, water covered the earth and destroyed the physical civilizations; there was darkness. This was the first flood—the flood of Lucifer.

2. From the Re-Creation to the Sin of Adam

The length of this time is undetermined but ended near 4004 BC. During this time, there must have been other beings of some type on the earth. We know the fallen angels were here because they were cast to the earth with Lucifer and remain here until the present time. Their activity and abilities were, of course, diminished after their fall; but nevertheless, they were and still are on the earth.

Adam and Eve were in the Garden. Adam was commanded to tend and keep the Garden but evidently, he allowed the serpent (Satan) to enter and spend time with his wife, Eve. Could it be that there were other nonhuman beings and creatures outside the Garden that could have lasted for many millennia, completely separate from the life of Adam and Eve? Is it possible that they, along with the assistance of the fallen angels, built some of the structures remaining to this day? Could it be?

3. After Adam Left the Garden (4004 BC) and Before the Flood of Noah (2348 BC)

From the time of Adam until the flood, 1,656 years had passed. During this time there were humans, the Watchers, fallen angels, and giants (Nephilim) on the earth.

4. After the Flood of Noah (2348 BC) until the Resurrection of Jesus

During this time there were humans, the angels of God, and fallen angels on the earth. The Nephilim (giants) existed at the beginning of this time until they were eliminated by the armies of Israel. The 200 Watchers were imprisoned at the time of the flood of Noah and were put in pits of darkness where they remain to this present day.

5. From the Resurrection of Jesus until Today

This time period is referred to as the age of grace, the church age, and the last days. During this time, born-again believers are called the sons of God, and they have been given authority over the power of the enemy. The redemption of humankind has been paid by the blood of the Lamb on the altar in heaven. This time period is from AD 30 until the present day. During this time period there are humans, the fallen angels, the Holy Spirit, and the angels of God on the earth.

Summary

After the original creation, there was a civilization on the earth. Within this earthly pre-Adamic civilization there were kings, kingdoms, and commerce (Ezekiel 28:16; Isaiah 14:12). We don't know for sure who the inhabitants were on the earth that made up these kingdoms. However, we do know that Lucifer was involved in trading with them. They may have been angelic and/or physical nonhuman beings, but it was not a civilization of human beings since Adam was the first man and he had not been yet placed in the Garden of Eden (1 Corinthians 15:45,47).

How long this civilization existed before Lucifer and one-third of the angels who followed him were cast down to the earth, we do not know. However, we do know there were kingdoms and obviously great structures built.

God, in His grace and mercy, put the earth back in order, created man, then placed him in the Garden, eastward in Eden. We are not told how long Adam lived in the Garden before he sinned and was expelled. But we do know this. The Bible gives us the genealogy of Jesus from His birth all the way back to Adam. This genealogy is in great detail, giving the age and years of every individual in the genealogy. That timeline can be accurately verified, and the result is this: Adam left the Garden 4,000 years before the birth of Jesus Christ.

After Adam left the Garden, as discussed previously, there was great sin and perversion on the earth, but God in His mercy cleansed the earth of evil with a flood. This flood at the time of Noah took place approximately 4,400 years ago in the year 2348 BC, which was approximately 1,656 years after Adam left the Garden.

So what does all this mean to us when we are trying to determine who built the ancient structures and how they did them? The answer is quite simple. If the structure was built after the flood of Noah, it was built by humans using the tools available. However, according to the Bible, there were Nephilim (giants) on the earth for several hundred years after the flood who most likely assisted in quarrying and moving the giant stones of some of the megalithic structures.

If the structure was built after Adam left the Garden but before the flood of Noah, according to the Bible, they could have been built by the Watchers, or giants, or humans, or a combination thereof.

Finally, if the structure is over 6,000 years old, it was obviously built before Adam left the Garden, and possibly during the time when the ancient civilizations, comprised of nonhuman beings and angels, were on the earth, but before the earth was covered by the waters in Genesis 1:2.

Because of centuries of indoctrination by religious institutions seeking to promote their doctrine and secular institutions teaching the Holy Bible is allegorical or only historical, the church in general has avoided confrontation with science. However, a deep study of Scripture will reveal truth. Sometimes this requires unlearning previous beliefs in order to come to the ultimate truth that is revealed in God's Word.

Chapter 6

ANGELS OF GOD

Any discussion of the spirit world would not be complete without exploring the existence of angels. Because of ancient fables, the teachings of cults and false religions, and ultimately fictional scripts written for theatrical and Hollywood productions, the accurate teaching about angels, their existence, and purpose has been skewed.

There are literally thousands of writings and references concerning angels. There are even ancient books pre-dating modern history that can be used as references. However, I would like to limit the absolute final authority of the following accounts concerning angels to one reference book—the Holy Bible.

So, join me as we dig deep into the truth and uncover the mystery of angels.

The Creation of Angels

Before the creation of man, God created the angels. They were magnificent, glorious creatures, filled with beauty and they worshiped God. There are different rankings in the angelic realm. There are archangels, seraphim, cherubim, living creatures, and other heavenly hosts. In ages past, all of the angels honored God Almighty with praise, worship, and music, fulfilling one of the duties of their creation.

The angels were present when God created man on Day 6 of creation. We know this from Psalm 8 when the angels observed what was going on and expressed awe that God was even mindful of man.

> *When I consider Your heavens, the work of Your fingers, the moon and the stars, which You have ordained, what is man that You are mindful of him, and the son of man that You visit him? For You have made him a little lower than the angels, and You have crowned him with glory and honor.*
>
> Psalm 8:3-5

Our English translations of Psalm 8:5 say, "a little lower than the angels," but the word there actually isn't angels. The Hebrew word is *elohim*. Genesis 1:1 uses the word *elohim* and it is translated, "In the beginning God." *Elohim* is translated "God" in the first verse of the Bible. As a matter of fact, out of the 2,606 times the word *elohim* is used in the Bible, Psalm 8:5 is the only time the translators translated the word as *angels*. So, the Bible really says that man was created a little lower than God, not a little lower than the angels.

God created man for a purpose, and He created angels for a purpose. Angels were never intended to be like God. They were created with a specific function, but that was not to be like God. God is very clear that He does not want mixing of seed. We are not referring to mixing races or nationalities or anything within the human race. All humans descended from Adam and are of one blood. God wants humans to stay within their domain, and angels to stay in their domain. Angels have a purpose and man has a purpose.

> *For to which of the angels did He ever say: "You are My Son, today I have begotten You"? And again: "I will be to Him a Father, and He shall be to Me a Son"?*
>
> HEBREWS 1:5

> *But to which of the angels has He ever said: "Sit at My right hand, till I make Your enemies Your footstool"?*
>
> HEBREWS 1:13

The Greek word *angelos* is transliterated into the English word *angels*, but the translation of *angelos* means "messenger." The definition of *angelos* in a biblical Greek to English dictionary says, "a messenger, envoy, one who is sent, an angel, a messenger from God."

Throughout the history of humankind, God has used angels as messengers. He sent a group of angels to give a message to the shepherds (Luke 2:8-14). He sent Gabriel to give a message to Zechariah the priest, the father of John the Baptist (Luke 1:11-20). He sent Gabriel again to enter the dream of Joseph with the message that he was to take Mary as his wife (Matthew 1:20).

When Were Angels Created?

First, we must acknowledge that angels have not always existed in the eons of time past. There was a point in time when they were created. We know this because the Bible tells us that Lucifer was perfect on the day he was created (Ezekiel 28:15). Simply put, this means that on the day before his creation, he did not exist. Unlike Almighty God, who has no beginning and has existed eternally beyond the ancient past, angels were created. The exact date they were created is unknown to us. However, we are given a general period of time that this creation took place.

Genesis 1:1 tells us God created the heavens and the earth in the beginning, and Isaiah 45:18 said this creation was perfect. It was not created formless and void but was created to be inhabited. We also find other references that the creations of God are good. Although currently there are angels of God and fallen angels, for an undetermined amount of time, they were all only good angels. Although some became bad, deformed, or evil, they were not created that way. Likewise, the heavens and the earth were created perfect and good. The Bible tells us that God is the giver of good and perfect gifts. What He creates is never chaotic or deformed.

> *Every good gift and every perfect gift is from above,*
> *and comes down from the Father of lights, with whom*
> *there is no variation or shadow of turning.*
> JAMES 1:17

Essentially there are two groups of angels on the earth today. In the first group are the angels of God that stayed loyal to God at the fall of Lucifer and did not participate in the sin of the Watchers. They can travel from the earth to the upper heavens and spend their time as messengers of God and ministers for those who will inherit salvation. They are by far in the majority (Hebrews 12:22).

When a person confesses that Jesus is Lord, the Lord Himself will in turn proclaim that confession to the angels of God on the day of judgment.

Also I say to you, whoever confesses Me before men, him the Son of Man also will confess before the angels of God.

LUKE 12:8

The second group of angels on the earth are the ones who fell with Lucifer when he was cast out of heaven. They are now evil spirits and devils just like their leader, Satan (Revelation 20:2). They are restricted from the presence of God.

A third group of angels that are no longer on the earth are the Watchers who are imprisoned in Tartarus until their day of judgment at the end of the millennium.

The Power of Angels Demonstrated

Throughout history, God has sent His angels to insert themselves into the lives of mankind, either as a response to a prayer, or to prepare an individual for a future plan of God in their life.

Some of these events may seem bizarre and even unbelievable, but we must never forget that angels move from the dimension of the unseen into our physical dimension here on earth at will. They can alter their appearance and change the laws of physics. We must remember nothing is impossible for God.

And He said to him, "Most assuredly, I say to you, hereafter you shall see heaven open, and the angels of God ascending and descending upon the Son of Man."

JOHN 1:51

When reading these biblical stories, it's tempting to relegate them to history or an event that can only happen to someone else. However, the people in the following stories were mere mortals just like you. Anything that God has done once, He can do again. And maybe, just maybe, there will be a supernatural intervention of an angelic presence in your life.

However, here is a caution. Never worship an angel or initiate communication directly with an angel (Colossians 2:18). As a Christian, our communication is with the Father, in the name of His Son, Jesus. Of course, if an angel is sent to bring a message, then a conversation would be permissible. But scripturally, we must remember that angels take messages from the throne of God to humans. They are angels of God—not angels of men. When we speak God's Word, His angels go forth to activate it. You are the voice of His word on the earth.

Bless the LORD, you His angels, who excel in strength, who do His word, heeding the voice of His word.

PSALM 103:20

The Power of One Prayer and One Angel

When King Hezekiah faced a military situation that looked like defeat, he prayed and God sent one angel. What happened? With that one prayer, the Lord sent one angel, and that angel alone killed 185,000 Assyrian soldiers in one night.

"Now, O LORD our God, rescue us from his power; then all the kingdoms of the earth will know that you alone, O LORD, are God" (2 Kings 19:19 NLT).

"That night the angel of the LORD went out to the Assyrian camp and killed 185,000 Assyrian soldiers. When the surviving Assyrians woke up the next morning, they found corpses everywhere" (2 Kings 19:35 NLT).

The Unseen Angelic Armies

When the king of Syria sent his great army to Dothan and surrounded Elisha and his servant, his servant was distressed. But Elisha told him that he should not fear, "for those who are with us are more than those who are with them" (2 Kings 6:16).

"And Elisha prayed, and said, 'LORD, I pray, open his eyes that he may see.' Then the LORD opened the eyes of the young man, and he saw. And behold, the mountain was full of horses and chariots of fire all around Elisha" (2 Kings 6:17).

Angels Inflict Blindness on Evil Men

Two angels were sent to Sodom to look for 10 righteous men so that the city would not be destroyed. Upon entering the city, the angels said they would spend the night in the open square. However, Lot (Abraham's nephew) asked them to stay in his house because he knew the wickedness of the city.

While the two angels were in Lot's house, the men of the city surrounded the house and called to Lot, saying, "Where are the men who came to you tonight? Bring them out to us that we may know them carnally" (Genesis 19:5). Lot, knowing the abomination of their desire, offered his daughters to them.

"But the two angels reached out, pulled Lot into the house, and bolted the door. Then they blinded all the men, young and old, who were at the door of the house, so they gave up trying to get inside" (Genesis 19:10-11 NLT).

Through this event, I am convinced that Lot learned a powerful lesson: The angels of God did not need his assistance.

The Fourth Man in the Fiery Furnace

Nebuchadnezzar was the king of Babylon and commanded everyone to worship the 90-foot gold statue he had built. Three Jews (Shadrach, Meshach, and Abed-Nego) refused to bow down and worship the image. God had forbidden it, and they knew God said He would be their deliverer. Nebuchadnezzar summoned the three men in order to give them one last chance to worship the statue, but they refused.

The king became full of rage and commanded his best soldiers to bind the three Hebrews and throw them into the furnace, which was heated to seven times its normal temperature. Shadrach, Meshach, and Abed-Nego fell down, bound, into the middle of the furnace. The soldiers who took the three men to the furnace were burned alive.

When the king looked into the fiery furnace, he saw the three Hebrew boys and a fourth figure, and asked: "'Did we not cast three men bound into the midst of the fire?' They answered and said to the king, 'True, O king.' 'Look!' he answered, 'I see four men loose, walking in the midst of the fire; and they are not hurt, and the form of the fourth is like the Son of God'" (Daniel 3:24-25).

This experience was so miraculous that Nebuchadnezzar praised God for sending His angel to rescue His servants who trusted in Him and then made this decree: "If any people, whatever their race or nation or language, speak a word against the God of Shadrach, Meshach, and Abed-Nego, they will be torn limb from limb, and their houses will be turned into heaps of rubble. There is no other god who can rescue like this!" (Daniel 3:29 NLT).

Angels Guarding the Tree of Life

In the Garden of Eden, God placed two trees—the tree of the knowledge of good and evil, and the tree of life. In the book of Revelation, we are told that the leaves of the tree of life bring healing (Revelation 22:2). When Adam sinned, his body was no longer an eternal body, but he became mortal and was expelled from the Garden. God told him that in that day, he would die. With a mortal body, the only way to have eternal life was by access to the tree of life, and God did not want Adam having eternal life in his fallen state. So God placed two angels east of Eden to keep fallen man from the tree of life until mankind could be redeemed.

> *Then the LORD God said, "Behold, the man has become like one of Us, to know good and evil. And now, lest he put out his hand and take also of the tree of life, and eat, and live forever"—therefore the LORD God sent him out of the garden of Eden to till the ground from which he was taken.*
>
> *So He drove out the man; and He placed cherubim at the east of the garden of Eden, and a flaming sword which turned every way, to guard the way to the tree of life.*
>
> GENESIS 3:22-24

It's interesting to note that after the Second Coming of Jesus and during the millennial reign of Christ on the earth, the nations that honor Israel will have full access to the leaves of the tree of life that will be in the heavenly Jerusalem.

> *Blessed are those who do His commandments, that they may have **the right to the tree of life**, and may enter through the gates into the city.*
>
> REVELATION 22:14

The nations that do not honor Israel during the millennium will be restricted from access to the leaves that bring healing.

This is a question I am often asked: If God said that Adam would die in that day, why did Adam live to be 930 years old? (Genesis 5:5). The answer is simply this. On the day Adam sinned, his covering (the glory of God) departed, and he realized he was naked. His spiritual death occurred at that moment and in God's way of timing, his physical body died in one day. The Bible tells us once in the Old Testament (Psalm 90:4), and once in the New Testament (2 Peter 3:8) that with God a day is a thousand years and a thousand years is a day. Adam physically died within God's day. He never made it to a thousand years (one day).

Angel Detained for Twenty-One Days

There is an unseen battle that takes place in the realm of the spirit when words are spoken in prayer. It's interesting to note that Psalm 103:20 says that angels are waiting to hear the voice of God's Word spoken. When Daniel spoke the will of God in prayer, an angel was dispatched to implement the answer to the prayer of Daniel.

"Then he said, 'Don't be afraid, Daniel. Since the first day you began to pray for understanding and to humble yourself before your God, your request has been heard in heaven. I have come in answer to your prayer. But for twenty-one days the spirit prince of the kingdom of Persia blocked my way. Then Michael, one of the archangels, came to help me, and I left him there with the spirit prince of the kingdom of Persia. Now I am here to explain what will happen to your people in the future, for this vision concerns a time yet to come'" (Daniel 10:12-14 NLT).

An observation of this verse implies that different angels have different powers. One angel battled for 21 days, but when Michael the archangel (Jude 1:9) arrived, the breakthrough occurred.

This is an example of how we should trust God—have faith in His promise—so deeply that we exercise patience, knowing that our words have been heard and the answer is on its way. There may be a battle being fought over our prayer in the spirit realm, but the angels of God always win as long as our words do not change, and we do not give up (1 John 5:15).

And let us not grow weary while doing good, for in due season we shall reap if we do not lose heart.
GALATIANS 6:9

Ezekiel's Encounter with the Living Creatures

Ezekiel was a priest who lived with the Jewish exiles in Babylon. He tells the story of a vision he had when he was 30 years old of a chariot and living creatures.

He described the creatures within the chariot with great detail: "From the center of the cloud came four living beings that looked human, except that each had four faces and four wings. Their legs were straight, and their feet had hooves like those of a calf and shone like burnished bronze. Under each of their four wings I could see human hands. So, each of the four beings had four faces and four wings" (Ezekiel 1:5-8 NLT).

"The wings of each living being touched the wings of the beings beside it. Each one moved straight forward in any direction without turning around. Each had a human face in the front, the face of a lion on the right side, the face of an ox on the left side, and the face of an eagle at the back. Each had two pairs of outstretched wings—one pair stretched out to touch the wings of the living beings on either side of it, and the other pair covered its body. They went in whatever direction the spirit chose, and they moved straight forward in any direction without turning around" (Ezekiel 1:9-12 NLT).

Evidently, the ultimate purpose of Ezekiel's vision was to deliver a message from the throne of God, once again showing that angels, regardless of their description, facilitate messages from God to man.

The four living creatures described by Ezekiel, and the four living creatures that the apostle John described in the book of Revelation are similar. They may not be the exact same beings, but they are definitely comparable and probably of the same order. These angels are an exalted order of angels whose primary purpose is worship (Revelation 19:4).

Before the throne there was a sea of glass, like crystal. And in the midst of the throne, and around the throne, were four living creatures full of eyes in front and in back. The first living creature was like a lion, the second living creature like a calf, the third living creature had a face like a man, and the fourth living creature was like a flying eagle. The four living creatures, each having six wings, were full of eyes around and within. And they do not rest day or night, saying: "Holy, holy, holy, Lord God Almighty, who was and is and is to come!"

REVELATION 4:6-8

When the Bible refers to living creatures in heaven, we can assume that there is great diversity simply from the ones described by the prophet Ezekiel. But with all this diversity, there is one thing in common: Everything was created by the Word of God.

An Angel Shut the Lions' Mouths

In the year 538 BC, a young Jewish boy named Daniel was taken from his homeland by the armies of King Nebuchadnezzar of Babylon. Daniel lived to the age of 90, and during his lifetime there were three kings in the kingdom of Babylon. During the reign of King Darius, Daniel found great favor with the king and was later appointed ruler over the entire region. Because of jealousy and an evil plot to prevent him from being appointed to a high office, Daniel was unjustly sentenced to be thrown into the lions' den. (Daniel 6.)

King Darius was forced to have Daniel thrown into a den of lions. But how did he survive? Daniel told the king, "My God sent His angel and shut the lions' mouths, so that they have not hurt me, because I was found innocent before Him; and also, O king, I have done no wrong before you" (Daniel 6:22).

The Angel Gabriel Visits Zechariah

Zechariah was the high priest and the father of John the Baptist. Zechariah and his wife, Elizabeth, were unable to have children. But one day while he was in the sanctuary performing priestly duties, an angel of the Lord appeared to him and said, "Don't be afraid, Zechariah! God has heard your prayer. Your wife, Elizabeth, will give you a son, and you are to name him John. You will have great joy and gladness, and many will rejoice at his birth" (Luke 1:13-14 NLT).

"Zechariah said to the angel, 'How can I be sure this will happen? I'm an old man now, and my wife is also well along in years.' Then the angel said, 'I am Gabriel! I stand in the very presence of God. It was He who sent me to bring you this good news! But now, since you didn't believe what I said, you will be silent and unable to speak until the child is born. For my words will certainly be fulfilled at the proper time'" (Luke 1:18-20 NLT).

The Angel Gabriel Visits Mary

When Elizabeth was in her sixth month of pregnancy, God sent the angel Gabriel to Nazareth to visit Mary.

"Gabriel appeared to her and said, 'Greetings, favored woman! The Lord is with you!'" (Luke 1:28 NLT).

Mary was troubled by this and tried to think what the angel could mean, but Gabriel told her to not be afraid. He went on to say that she had found favor with God and would conceive and give birth to a son named Jesus.

"Mary asked the angel, 'But how can this happen? I am a virgin.' The angel replied, 'The Holy Spirit will come upon you, and the power of the Most High will overshadow you.' Mary responded, 'I am the Lord's servant. May everything you have said about me come true.' And then the angel left her" (Luke 1:34-35,38 NLT).

An Angel Entered Joseph's Dream

The Bible says that in the latter days there will be an increase in prophetic dreams (Acts 2:17). When Joseph learned Mary was pregnant and decided to quietly call off the wedding, a very extraordinary thing happened. The Bible says that an angel actually entered into his dream. He didn't have a dream about an angel, but an angel somehow entered into a different dimension and delivered a message.

"But while he thought about these things, behold, an angel of the Lord appeared to him in a dream, saying, 'Joseph, son of David, do not be afraid to take to you Mary your wife, for that which is conceived in her is of the Holy Spirit'" (Matthew 1:20).

It's interesting to note that this is not the first time in Scripture that an angel appeared in a dream to deliver a message. This also happened to Jacob in Genesis 31:10-13.

Angels Praise God at the Birth of Jesus

Angels praise and worship God throughout the heavens and around the throne. However, one place recorded in Scripture where the angels praised God on earth was at the announcement to the shepherds of the birth of Jesus. One can only imagine the glory and splendor of that event.

And suddenly there was with the angel a multitude of the heavenly host praising God and saying: "Glory to God in the highest, and on earth peace, goodwill toward men!"

LUKE 2:13-14

Peter Rescued from Prison

Angels are ministering spirits sent to minister for the saints. They are not slaves sent to perform mundane tasks for us. Angels will assist a believer with the impossible, but will not cut your grass because you are too lazy to do it.

We see a great example of this when Peter was in prison awaiting trial. The Roman soldiers who were guarding him knew that if Peter escaped, they would receive his punishment. With this knowledge, they made sure that Peter was securely bound. He was fastened with two chains between two soldiers and more guards were at the prison gate.

"Suddenly, there was a bright light in the cell, and an angel of the Lord stood before Peter. The angel struck him on the side to awaken him and said, 'Quick! Get up!' And the chains fell off his wrists. Then the angel told him, 'Get dressed and put on your sandals.' And he did. 'Now put on your coat and follow me,' the angel ordered. So Peter left the cell, following the angel. But all the time he thought it was a vision. He didn't realize it was actually happening. They passed the first and second guard posts and came to the iron gate leading to the city, and this opened for them all by itself. So they passed through and started walking down the street, and then the angel suddenly left him" (Acts 12:7-10 NLT).

Peter could not loosen the chains, get past the guards, or open the gate, but the angel could and did. However, Peter had to get dressed, put on his own sandals, and follow instructions. Obviously, the angel would do what Peter couldn't do, but wouldn't do what Peter could do.

An Angel Appeared to Paul

The Bible says that many unusual miracles took place at the hands of Paul (Acts 19:11). In most places today, any miracle would be unusual. But the statement that Paul had unusual miracles take place in his life indicates that normal miracles were a common event.

It's interesting to note that Paul was visited by angels that would advise him and give him advance knowledge of events that were to take place in the future. We must remember that Paul lived in the same dispensation that we are in today, governed by the same rules and regulations. This means that anything that happened through Paul—miracles, visitations, or conversations with angels—can happen to any born-again Christian today.

> *For there stood by me this night an angel of the God to whom I belong and whom I serve.*
>
> Acts 27:23

Three Angels Preach the Gospel During the Great Tribulation

During the seven-year period, known as the Great Tribulation, which takes place between the rapture of the church and the Second Coming, the desire of God's heart does not change. Even though the church will be taken away for the judgment seat of Christ and the marriage supper of the Lamb in heaven, God still desires for those who are left behind to be saved from hell.

While the antichrist is attempting to set up his kingdom, there will be 144,000 young Jewish men (12,000 from each Israeli tribe) sent out to preach the gospel of the kingdom throughout the earth. There will be two witnesses proclaiming the truth and likewise angels will be dispatched proclaiming the gospel to all. The three angels of Revelation 14 are an example of this.

First Angel Preaches the Gospel

"And I saw another angel flying through the sky, carrying the eternal Good News to proclaim to the people who belong to this world—to every nation, tribe, language, and people. 'Fear God,' he shouted. 'Give glory to Him. For the time has come when He will sit as judge. Worship Him who made the heavens, the earth, the sea, and all the springs of water'" (Revelation 14:6-7 NLT).

Second Angel Proclaims the Defeat of Babylon

"Then another angel followed him through the sky, shouting, 'Babylon is fallen—that great city is fallen—because she made all the nations of the world drink the wine of her passionate immorality'" (Revelation 14:8 NLT).

Third Angel Warns of Taking the Mark of the Beast

"Then a third angel followed them, shouting, 'Anyone who worships the beast and his statue or who accepts his mark on the forehead or on the hand must drink the wine of God's anger. It has been poured full strength into God's cup of wrath. And they will be tormented with fire and burning sulfur in the presence of the holy angels and the Lamb. The smoke of their torment will rise forever and ever, and they will have no relief day or night, for they have worshiped the beast and his statue and have accepted the mark of his name'" (Revelation 14:9-11 NLT).

Angels Worship in the Throne Room of Heaven

The center of the known universe and the unknown expanse of creation—and beyond—is the throne of God. Absolutely nothing compares, competes, or challenges the throne room. If anyone would ask what God desires, the answer can be profoundly revealed by this. He surrounds Himself with His greatest desire. What does God bring into His presence? What surrounds His throne? Innumerable angels, living beings, elders, and the saints of God, who are all praising and worshiping the Lamb that redeemed mankind.

When one ponders the importance of angels in God's kingdom, we only need to understand this reality. Throughout eternity in the throne room of heaven, the angels will be present.

> *...I heard the voice of many angels around the throne, the living creatures, and the elders; and the number of them was ten thousand times ten thousand, and thousands of thousands, saying with a loud voice: "Worthy is the Lamb who was slain to receive power and riches and wisdom, and strength and honor and glory and blessing!"*
>
> REVELATION 5:11-12

How Does the Existence of God's Angels Affect Us Today?

As mentioned earlier in this chapter, there are two groups of angels on the earth in this current dispensation of time—the angels of God and fallen angels. The angels of God are here to assist the church of God. As a Christian, you should never forget that the Bible says that God's angels are here to assist you in doing God's will for your life. The Bible gives us the mission statement of His angels during this dispensation: "Are they not all ministering spirits sent forth to minister for those who will inherit salvation?" (Hebrews 1:14).

The second group of angels on the earth are the fallen angels. They are in opposition and are the enemy of God and the church. Their mission statement is listed in John 10:10 where it says their goal is to steal, kill, and to destroy. However, the church has been given authority over this group of fallen spirits, and if a Christian takes the authority that was given, the enemy must flee.

> *Behold, I give you the authority to trample on serpents and scorpions, and over all the power of the enemy, and nothing shall by any means hurt you.*
>
> LUKE 10:19

> *Therefore submit to God. Resist the devil and he will flee from you.*
>
> JAMES 4:7

In conclusion, the angels of God are here to assist Christians, and Christians have been given authority over the devil and his fallen angels.

Chapter 7

UFOs and the Bible

The first movie about traveling through space was called *A Trip to the Moon*, a French adventure silent film created in 1902. The subject of the movie was a group of astronomers who traveled to the moon, escaped from the lunar inhabitants (Selenites), and returned to earth with a captured Selenite.

In 1951, the first talking movie involving aliens was released and since then thousands of movie scripts have been written about spaceships, aliens, and traveling through space.

For centuries, people have been seeing things in the sky. In fact, there are paintings dating back hundreds of years that show images in the sky with little beings inside the craft. People called them "little green men."

But in 2021, the U.S. government began disclosing reports on UFOs saying they have all types of military information about them. The military says they have actually tracked these devices and that many of them can go from a standing still position to 10,000 miles per hour in a split second.

This lets us know there are no humans inside these crafts, because they would be pulverized from the G-force. Mankind cannot live in an environment that moves from nothing to 10,000 miles per hour in a split second.

Recently, a military pilot with several jet fighters under his command was on a training mission when they spotted a UFO and tracked it on their radar. It was being tracked from the ground as well for an extended period of time. The pilot finally decided he would dive down to take a look at it up close to see what it was. Everything was recorded on equipment in his plane; but when he got close to the craft, instantly it was gone.

What was once considered fantasy is now being considered reality by some of the leading scientists and political leaders of our day. Military and political leaders are now speaking openly concerning these unexplained objects that are appearing in the sky.

Unidentified Anomalous Phenomena—UAP

The United States Air Force coined the acronym "UFO" in 1952. On June 24, 1947, Kenneth Arnold, a private pilot, said he saw unidentified flying objects in the sky near Mount Rainier. Shortly after his observation, it was reported that a flying disc had crashed near Roswell, New Mexico. That set off a national craze of "flying saucers," and the term "UFO" became a cultural phenomenon.

The term "UFO" became so popular that many movies and documentaries used it to stand for any flying object that was unidentified. During the 1990s, most of the public felt that the government was covering up information about UFOs. A very popular TV series called *The X-Files* exploited this theory in their episodes and further fueled what the government called a conspiracy theory.

The term "UAP" was first used in 1987 at the "International Symposium on Unidentified Aerial Phenomena" that met on the 40th anniversary of the Roswell incident. The United States Pentagon established a Navy-led "UAP Task Force" to investigate reports of UAPs.

Gradually through the years, the term UFO became so associated with conspiracy theories, science fiction, and fantasy that when someone mentioned a UFO, it was usually followed by a smirk and a rolling of the eyes. Many pilots kept their encounters private because they did not want to face humiliation and ridicule.

Because of the stigma associated with the term UFO, NASA and the US government officially changed their terminology from UFO to UAP. Later the term UAP, which originally stood for Unidentified Aerial Phenomena, was changed to Unidentified Anomalous Phenomena because many of the unidentified objects were also seen entering the oceans.

Government Disclosure

In recent years, the United States federal government has disclosed through press releases and congressional hearings that UFOs do exist. In one recent congressional hearing, it was disclosed that hundreds of military and commercial pilots have reported UFO encounters. The Pentagon released several videos showing these objects.

One military pilot testified before Congress that he was close enough to a UFO that he could see it had no obvious means of propulsion, and its frame did not contain rivets. He stated that as he watched, it instantly disappeared and moments later showed up on military radar 60 miles away. The disclosure of UFOs has now been moved from hidden back rooms to the forefront for the public to view.

NASA has stated that one of its key priorities is the search for life elsewhere in the universe. As of this writing, NASA has not found any credible evidence of extraterrestrial life and there is no evidence that UFOs are extraterrestrial. Why are UFOs never seen beyond the atmosphere of earth? It's interesting to note that Satan and the fallen angels are restricted to the earth and its atmosphere (the first heaven), and they are not allowed to leave. Could there be a connection?

The question is no longer do UFOs exist, but rather what are they? As Christians, we must be informed so that when we are approached with questions about UFOs by people outside the church, we can give an intelligent answer that is supported by a biblical narrative.

Desensitizing the Public

As a Christian, we have to determine in our hearts a reality of how this plays out with the Word of God, and what it means to us. We are in what I call a "time of disclosure," and there's a purpose behind this. We are gradually being told in the media that aliens exist, and they are benevolent.

We have been shown in movies what "wisdom they have." Everyone knows the wisdom of Yoda, the fictional character from *Star Wars*. Yoda was not created in the image and likeness of God; his character was created in Hollywood.

Yoda's character is fictional, but is perceived as a possible reality in further desensitizing the public to the possibility that aliens truly do exist in other forms. Even though fictional, the concept of alien life being real gets into people's belief systems. We are being told through movies that there are other creations that interact with us in a peaceful way, if we will allow them. This is propaganda!

Although they are frequently portrayed as adorable, they have a much darker side. Grey aliens or "Grays" are frequent subjects in claims of alien abductions. There are countless documentaries of human abductions by aliens and their accounts are very similar. Many report medical experiments being performed on them before they are returned. Although memory loss is a common side effect, the memories that return follow a uniform pattern among those who have been taken.

Communicating with Aliens

Second Corinthians 11:14 says, "Satan himself transforms himself into an angel of light." The Contemporary English Version of the Bible translates it, "Even Satan tries to make himself look like an angel of light."

Second Corinthians 11:15 (ESV) tells us, "So it is no surprise if his servants, also, disguise themselves as servants of righteousness."

There are mediums who claim to communicate with spirits and aliens through séances, channeling, automatic writing, and other various means. These people who are talking to "aliens" are actually speaking to demonic spirits who are attempting, through deception, to keep people from knowing the truth.

If the devil can cause a person to place their faith in the existence of extraterrestrials (beings from outer space), then it dilutes their faith in God.

First Corinthians 12:10 tells us one of the gifts of the Holy Spirit is "discerning of spirits." Why would we need to discern spirits if all the spirits talking are good? No, we need discerning of spirits because there are spirits appearing to be good that are not. That's what deception is. Deception means that the person being deceived doesn't think they are being deceived; they think they're right.

> *Give no regard to mediums and familiar spirits; do not seek after them, to be defiled by them: I am the LORD your God.*
> LEVITICUS 19:31

We know that one-third of the heavenly hosts rebelled against God, and God cast them down to the earth and to the air around the earth. The atmosphere around the earth (everything up to the tallest mountain) was considered to be the first heaven by the Hebrews and even by the ancient Greeks.

When the Bible says the enemy is the prince of the power of the air (Ephesians 2:2), he is not in God's heaven, he is in the first heaven (the atmosphere) of earth. He is part of the principalities and powers of the air. That is who we wrestle against (Ephesians 6:12).

To use a medium to contact "aliens" is not only futile, but in the end will bring defilement. These so-called aliens are actually familiar (fallen) spirits and should be avoided. To place credibility in this form of communication is not only unproductive, but it is unbiblical.

I spoke to a young man who said he'd been abducted by aliens, the Grays. He had not even told his parents about it but wanted to meet with me to find out what I thought. He said, "They were some of the most loving creatures out there, and it really didn't hurt a lot when they injected the needles into me."

The young man is deceived. There is nothing in the Bible that speaks of angels abducting humans and performing medical experiments. Medical experiments by alien beings will always be orchestrated by the kingdom of darkness. Why would God need to experiment on a being He created?

What Does the Bible Say?

While earthly knowledge is increasing daily, I am again reminded of this truth: True scientific knowledge and true biblical Scripture do not disagree; rather, with every true scientific discovery, the Holy Scriptures are proven to be accurate.

Man's natural knowledge of the cosmos is increasing at a rate beyond our ability to process.

So with this in mind, let's examine what the Bible has to say about ariel craft, alien beings, and abductions—because we can always learn when we access the unlimited knowledge in God's Word.

First, let's take a look at Ephesians 6:11-12: "Put on the whole armor of God, that you may be able to stand against the wiles of the devil. For we do not wrestle against flesh and blood, but against principalities, against powers, against the rulers of the darkness of this age, against spiritual hosts of wickedness in the heavenly places."

There are some questions that must be answered. Are these beings that are involved in the sightings good, or are they evil? That can't be answered by yes or no because it depends on who it is, and which being it is. Some beings from the spirit realm represent God, which are messengers, angels, or angelic beings. But some beings from the spirit world do not represent God. They are the principalities, powers, rulers of the darkness of this age, and spiritual hosts of wickedness.

In 2 Corinthians 11:3, Paul told us that as Eve was deceived in the Garden by the serpent's clever lies, he didn't want our thoughts to be corrupted from the simplicity that is in Christ. That does not mean that Christ is simple. It just means that the gospel He teaches is not complicated. God is easy to understand regardless of someone's intellectual level.

Throughout history past and in biblical prophetic writings, there have been and will be signs and wonders in the sky that are from God. Their purpose will always be for good and for the benefit of the saints. With that in mind, let's take a look at several biblical accounts of never-before-seen objects in the sky.

The Wheel Within the Wheel

Ezekiel the prophet had an encounter with some kind of unidentified object that no one had ever seen before. The following is an account in his own words:

"Then I looked, and behold, a whirlwind was coming out of the north, a great cloud with raging fire engulfing itself; and brightness was all around it and radiating out of its midst like the color of amber, out of the midst of the fire. Also, from within it came the likeness of four living creatures. And this was their appearance: they had the likeness of a man" (Ezekiel 1:4-5).

"As for the likeness of the living creatures, their appearance was like burning coals of fire, like the appearance of torches going back and forth among the living creatures. The fire was bright, and out of the fire went lightning. And the living creatures ran back and forth, in appearance like a flash of lightning. Now as I looked at the living creatures, behold, a wheel was on the earth beside each living creature with its four faces. The appearance of the wheels and their workings…" (Ezekiel 1:13-16).

The Hebrew word used for "the appearance of the wheels and their workings" is *merkabah*, which is the same word the Israelis use for their military tanks. The fact that it says, *"and their workings*" implies that it is mechanical. Ask yourself this question: Why would spirits (or angels) from heaven need anything mechanical?

"The appearance of the wheels and their workings was like the color of beryl, and all four had the same likeness. The appearance of their workings was, as it were, a wheel in the middle of a wheel" (Ezekiel 1:16).

Could it be that when Ezekiel saw this, it was like nothing he had ever seen before? He said there was a wheel within a wheel. The New Living Translation version says, "each wheel had a second wheel turning crosswise within it."

A favorite toy from my childhood was a gyroscope. It had a spinning wheel within a wheel. A gyroscope is defined as a spinning wheel or disc in which the axis of rotation (spin action) is free to assume any orientation by itself. It has made possible many modern devices including the inertial navigation systems such as are in the Hubble Space Telescope and inside the steel hull of a submerged submarine.

When Ezekiel is talking about the wheel in the middle of a wheel, he is using the best verbiage he can use for the day he lived in.

Like on the day of Pentecost, the Bible says there was the sound of a rushing mighty wind in the upper room. It doesn't say there *was* a rushing mighty wind. It says there was *the sound as* a rushing mighty wind. Why didn't they say it sounded like a jet turbine? Because they didn't know what a jet turbine engine was. Ezekiel described the wheel the best way he could within the context of what he knew.

Ezekiel continued in his description of this flying object by saying, "When they moved, they went toward any one of four directions; they did not turn aside when they went. As for their rims, they were so high they were awesome; and their rims were full of eyes, all around the four of them" (Ezekiel 1:17-18).

"When the living creatures went, the wheels went beside them; and when the living creatures were lifted up from the earth, the wheels were lifted up. Wherever the spirit wanted to go, they went, because there the spirit went; and the wheels were lifted together with them, for the spirit of the living creatures was in the wheels. When those went, these went, when those stood, these stood; and when those were lifted up from the earth, the wheels were lifted up together with them, for the spirit of the living creatures was in the wheels" (Ezekiel 1:19-21).

So, what was it that Ezekiel saw? It was definitely something unidentified. It was flying and it was difficult for him to explain with the limited knowledge of technology he had in his generation. In modern terms, we could say he experienced an encounter with a UFO.

The Flying Scroll

I looked up again and saw a scroll flying through the air.

ZECHARIAH 5:1 NLT

Through the centuries there have been numerous artist's renditions of the flying scroll described by Zechariah through paintings, murals, and even stained glass. As I looked at these images, they most often portrayed long tubular objects, and some were even disc shaped.

> *"What do you see?" the angel asked. "I see a flying scroll," I replied. "It appears to be about 30 feet long and 15 feet wide."*
> ZECHARIAH 5:2 NLT

What he saw was in the shape of a scroll, which was something he was familiar with. What was it that Zechariah saw? Someone seeing the same thing today might say, "I saw a UFO."

Chariots of Fire

On a certain day Elijah and Elisha were together. As they were walking and talking, suddenly a chariot of fire with horses of fire separated them and Elijah was taken up by a whirlwind into heaven. As discussed earlier with Ezekiel's encounter, the prophets of old could only describe what they saw using the culture and knowledge they possessed. Likewise, Elijah described what he saw using the knowledge he had. Could it be that what he saw was a mechanical craft? Could this further validate the thought that there is technology in God's kingdom?

> *Then it happened, as they continued on and talked, that suddenly a chariot of fire appeared with horses of fire, and separated the two of them; and Elijah went up by a whirlwind into heaven.*
> 2 KINGS 2:11

Why was a chariot needed, and why was it called a chariot of fire when the chariots they had at that time did not have fire? Earthly chariots had wheels and were pulled along by earthly horses. So, what was the fire they were seeing? Obviously, the horses were not physical. You have to understand that Elijah was describing what he saw using terminology he was familiar with. This encounter lets us know that there are traveling devices that come from heaven.

More Chariots of Fire

"Now the king of Syria was making war against Israel; and he consulted with his servants, saying, 'My camp will be in such and such a place'" (2 Kings 6:8).

Every time the king of Syria would plan an attack against Israel, Israel knew of the attack in advance, so they either avoided a battle, or were victorious in battle. The king of Syria became suspicious and thought he could possibly have a spy within his own camp. One of his assistants told the king, "There is a prophet in Israel who tells the king of Israel the words you speak even in your bedroom" (2 Kings 6:12). So the king of Syria sent his army to capture Elisha.

"Therefore he sent horses and chariots and a great army there, and they came by night and surrounded the city. And when the servant of the man of God arose early and went out, there was an army surrounding the city with horses and chariots. And his servant said to him, 'Alas, my master! What shall we do?' So he answered, 'Do not fear, for those who are with us are more than those who are with them'" (2 Kings 6:14-16).

It's understandable that Elisha's servant was fearful. After all, the Syrian army surrounded the city where they were staying. The situation looked hopeless when Elisha the prophet made the profound statement that there were more with them than there were with the Syrians. This obviously brought great confusion to the servant because he could see the Syrian army, and only he and Elisha stood against them. Then Elisha asked the Lord to open the eyes of his servant and the servant could see into the spiritual realm. What did he see? The mountain was full of horses and chariots of fire all around Elisha.

> *And Elisha prayed, and said, "LORD, I pray, open his eyes that he may see." Then the LORD opened the eyes of the young man, and he saw. And behold, the mountain was full of horses and chariots of fire all around Elisha.*
>
> 2 KINGS 6:17

This encounter raises more questions. Obviously, the chariots of fire being drawn by horses had soldiers in them. Horses and chariots alone could not do battle; soldiers are required. Who were the soldiers? Once again, obviously they were angels sent from heaven. But why did they need chariots and why did the chariots need something (horses) to draw them? When the servant had his eyes opened, he saw into the spiritual dimension, and he saw that the soldiers of God (angels) used technology in their travel to the place of battle. The prophet Ezekiel was taken up in a chariot of fire, and here we see chariots of fire again.

Satan Imitates, But It's a Counterfeit

When Moses went up on the mountain for 40 days, the Bible tells us that everything that was to be in the tabernacle was shown to him in heaven as a pattern so that he would know what to build when he descended from the mountain (Hebrews 8:5). In other words, earth is a pattern of heaven. What we have in the visible realm exists in the invisible realm, only what we have is a scaled-down, cut-back, imitation version.

When Jesus put His blood on the ark of the covenant, He put His blood on the original ark of the covenant in heaven, not the imitation on earth made with human hands. The one on earth had the blood of bulls and goats put on it for a long time. The one in heaven never had blood placed on it. The ark in heaven was waiting for the perfect blood so the perfect sacrifice could be placed on the perfect altar. On earth was the imitation, which was the earthly altar made out of earthly substances with earthly blood on it.

By taking the sum of the scriptures in the Holy Bible, it can be observed that what is on the earth is a physical replication or image of what is in heaven.

Could it be that the chariots the Syrians were using on earth were just imitations of the magnificent chariots that are in heaven? Could the enemy try to imitate and copy in order to draw us away from the original?

The reason there are so many false religions on the earth is because the enemy makes a counterfeit of everything that God does.

In the past, I have served on the board of directors of several banking institutions. Do you know how to recognize counterfeit currency? You study the real currency and become so familiar with it that when you see the counterfeit currency, you easily recognize it as fake. That's what Christians need to do. We must study the Word of God and know it so well that when a false teaching arises, we can easily recognize the deception. God is not the author of confusion but of peace. And when things seem confusing, it's not of God (1 Corinthians 14:33).

Do Not Fear

For God has not given us a spirit of fear, but of power,
and of love and of a sound mind.

2 TIMOTHY 1:7

Never forget that some things seen in the sky are not evil. Some objects, spirits, and manifestations are of God and submit to the will of God. However, there are objects, spirits, and manifestations that are not of God, whose purpose is to prevent the will of God. Discerning of spirits is the method God placed in the church during this dispensation to know the difference.

We rejoice as God moves through His Holy Spirit in these last days, but we should never fear the enemy. Rather, once the enemy is identified, we take the authority we have been given as the church and rebuke and resist the forces of evil.

Therefore submit to God. Resist the devil and he will
flee from you.

JAMES 4:7

Do not be afraid of a UFO. If a little Grey alien appears to you and says, "Take me to your leader!" You should say, "I rebuke you in the name of Jesus!"

"Nevertheless, do not rejoice in this, that the spirits are subject to you" (Luke 10:20). In other words, don't go on a demon hunt. Do you know how many demons are here on earth? Here's the answer—the same amount that were here in Jesus' time. They have all been cast out many times. When you cast out a demon, it's still here roaming the earth looking for a place to land. Just keep your own house clear.

> *When an unclean spirit goes out of a man, he goes through dry places, seeking rest, and finds none.*
> MATTHEW 12:43

Jesus says in Luke 10:19, "Behold, I give you the authority to trample on serpents and scorpions and over all the power of the enemy and nothing shall by any means hurt you."

The Unseen Spiritual Forces of Faith and Fear

Faith and fear are the two forces in the spirit realm that activate angelic assistance. Faith activates the angels of God, and fear activates fallen angels (demonic spirits). Romans 10:17 says that faith comes by hearing when you hear the Word of God. To activate faith, you must hear and believe what God says.

Likewise, fear comes from hearing, but it comes by hearing the words of the enemy. When you hear and believe what he says, it activates fear.

Faith and fear are opposites. In the same way that hot and cold, up and down, east and west are opposites, likewise faith and fear are opposites. They cannot both be active at the same time.

In my airplane, there is a gauge that gives me the rate of ascent or the rate of descent. It tells me how quickly I am ascending, or how quickly I am descending. There is only one gauge for this function because I cannot be doing both at the same time. If I am going up, I am not going down. And if I am going down, I am not going up. Up and down are opposites, and you cannot be doing both at the same time. It is the same way with faith and fear.

Psalm 103:20 says that angels (the angels of God) are mighty in strength, and they are standing by waiting to hear the voice of God's Word. When they hear it, they act upon it. As a Christian, you are the voice of God's Word on the earth today. When you say what He says, it activates His angels to minister for you in the area of the promise in His Word that you have believed and spoken. In other words, when you say and confess what God says about you, it activates the angels of God to bring it to pass.

Fear is a spirit, and it is not sent from God. The enemy uses fear to paralyze, immobilize, and render our faith useless. Terror, bad reports, and all negative words are for the purpose of developing fear. When you believe and speak the negative words of fear, these words fuel the demonic realm. By relinquishing your authority that comes through the words of faith, you, by default, allow the enemy to bring destruction.

God's Word says you can do all things through Christ who strengthens you (Philippians 4:13), but if the words coming out of your mouth are, "I can't do this. We are going to be destroyed. There's no hope for us," you will nullify the authority you've been given over the power of the enemy. And you open the door for the enemy to enter your house through fear.

Do UFOs exist? Yes, there is conclusive evidence that they exist; they are real. But you have not been given a spirit of fear, so do not respond to fear. When you hear words of terror and disaster, do not fear. Remember Psalm 91:7. Speak it and let it become *rhema* in your heart: "A thousand may fall at your side, and ten thousand at your right hand; but it shall not come near you."

Why Are They Doing What They're Doing?

To summarize, the players that are on earth right now are the angels of God, the fallen angels (demons), Satan, mankind, the church, and, of course, the Holy Spirit. So who is orchestrating the manifestations of unidentified objects flying in the atmosphere and into the oceans of the earth?

Since the Roswell incident, the secular world has been pushing the concept that UFOs are alien entities from outer space or other dimensions. It has even been suggested that in the ancient past, the earth was seeded with humans and the aliens have been periodically returning to inspect the progress. It has been proposed by some that the reported abductions of humans by the aliens are merely physical inspections of the progress of mankind.

Why would the secular world promote this? Could the underlying reason be the enemy wants to have an explanation ready to implement when the church is caught up and taken to heaven as prophesied in 1 Thessalonians 4:16? In order to keep those remaining on the earth after the rapture under his control, there must be an explanation for this mass abduction. Could his excuse simply be that it was aliens instead of Jesus?

UFOs of the Future

It is prophesied in the Bible that in the end of days it would be as in the days of Noah (Luke 17:26). We know that in the days of Noah there was great evil on the earth perpetrated by the forces of darkness. That can be expected as we approach the time of the return of Jesus. But likewise, it is prophesied that in the end of days there will be signs and wonders in the heavens.

> *I will show wonders in heaven above and signs in the earth beneath: blood and fire and vapor of smoke.*
> ACTS 2:19

For the person living in this dispensation at the close of the end of days, great discernment must be exercised. As God performs wonders, likewise Satan attempts to imitate them, making himself seem benevolent.

When Moses threw down his staff and it became a serpent, Pharaoh's magicians also threw down their staffs, which also became serpents. Satan cannot create anything; he only attempts to duplicate with deception. Living in the end of days we must clearly discern whether the things we see are like the serpent of Moses or the serpent of Pharaoh's magicians. Remember, on the floor they all looked the same, but they weren't. The staff that became a serpent when Moses threw it to the ground swallowed the serpents of the magicians.

> *For false christs and false prophets will rise and show great signs and wonders to deceive, if possible, even the elect.*
>
> MATTHEW 24:24

Do not be led astray by what looks right—be led by discerning of spirits furnished by the Holy Spirit so you will know the truth and not be led into deception. Remember, it's not what you see that sets you free, it's knowing the truth that sets you free (John 8:32).

So when it comes to seeing something in the sky that you cannot identify, always remember that the fallen angels are not the only ones at work in the end of days; angels of God are traveling through portals back and forth from heaven doing the work of God on the earth (John 1:51).

Chapter 8

TIME TRAVEL

The concept of a time machine has been the foundation of many science fiction novels and movies; but in the world of real science, is time travel into the distant past or into the distant future even possible?

We live in a world where people generally believe our lives are governed by time. People believe that time is a constant, and that time is the same for everyone. It seems to govern everything we do. But modern science tells us that time is a variable, not a constant.

We are all "time travelers" in that we travel forward in time from one hour to the next, and from one birthday to the next. All travel through time seems to be in forward motion for everyone, and all of humanity travels at the same rate with no one progressing further into the future than anyone else. We all use the same calendar. However, time does seem to progress faster as we get older.

Is there a place where time is moving slower or faster than time as we know it? Is there a place where time literally stops or even moves in reverse? Is there a place where time becomes divided into multiple timelines? Can we even imagine this? What does the Bible say? Does the Bible suggest that time is changeable?

Does Time Really Exist or Is It an Illusion?

In the 4ᵗʰ century, there was a heretic who later became a Christian bishop, and his name was Augustine. He wrote a paper that has some modern physicists scratching their heads. He said time comes in three phases—time past, time future, and time present. He said time past is gone, time future hasn't happened yet, and time present takes up exactly no space, concluding time doesn't exist. It's only an illusion.

We know Augustine was wrong because the Bible clearly tells us time has a beginning and an end.

Sir Isaac Newton said that time existed in and of itself separate from any outside influence. But later he discovered he was wrong about that, and we know now that wasn't the truth.

How Time Works According to Einstein

More than a century ago, Albert Einstein developed a hypothesis of how time works. He called it "relativity." In his theory, he concluded that time and space are linked together. Interestingly, he also said that our universe has a speed limit, and that nothing could travel faster than the speed of light, which is 186,282 miles per second.

So how does Albert Einstein's theory affect our view of time travel? According to his theory, the faster you travel, the slower you experience time. There have been many scientific experiments that prove this to be true.

As an example, two atomic clocks were set to the exact same time. One clock stayed on the earth and the other was put in a jet that flew in the same direction as the earth's rotation. After this flight around the world, the clocks were compared, and the clock on the airplane was slightly behind the clock that remained on the ground. Although we're dealing in nanoseconds (the smallest calculable period of time), nevertheless time was altered. The conclusion is time is not a constant, but it is relative to speed. In theory, as an object increases in speed, time decreases.

Einstein's second theory is that time itself is also actually relative to gravity. He theorized that gravity could curve space and time causing the passage of time to slow down. The pull of earth's gravity decreases with its distance from earth. His discovery was confirmed when our space capsules that traveled around the moon came back and the atomic clocks were compared. This verified that there is a difference in time when gravity is inserted into the equation. It is now known that gravity affects time.

Black Holes and Infinity

A few months ago, I was reading in *Scientific Weekly* about black holes, which in the past we didn't believe existed. But for the past 25 years it has been known that they actually are real. If you read old scientific journals, they will say black holes are just a theory. They are no longer a theory, they do exist.

It has been discovered that the farthest black hole in the universe still has gravitational pull all the way to earth. Some scientists think that gravity itself can be infinite. If time is infinite, gravity is infinite, light is infinite, and eternity is infinite, this brings new revelation to the reality that God is an infinite God and is the Creator of infinite things.

Muons and Time Alteration

A *muon* is an unstable subatomic particle. About 10,000 muons reach every square meter of the earth's surface every minute. These charged particles form as by-products of cosmic rays colliding with molecules in the upper atmosphere. They travel at realistic speeds. They can penetrate tens of meters of rock and other matter before they dissolve. Here's the point. They only exist for two millionths of a second, or 2.2 microseconds.

If they only exist for 2.2 microseconds and they are not traveling at the speed of light (but close to it), how can they survive coming through our atmosphere from outer space, and then penetrate into the ground? That takes much more than 2.2 microseconds. Science has quibbled over that dilemma for years. Then they discovered this reality. Because the muons are traveling so close to the speed of light, time is altered for them. And what 2.2 microseconds is to us is not 2.2 microseconds to them. This tends to validate Einstein's theory of relativity.

Time Variations

Clyde McGee was an aerospace engineer and a personal friend. Many years ago, he was given the task of engineering a way for a satellite (orbiting 24,000 miles above the earth) to remain in synchronous orbit—which would allow instantaneous worldwide communication. His research cleared the path for the development of our Global Positioning System (GPS). He was a deeply spiritual man who gave God the credit for his discoveries.

Currently, NASA scientists use high-accuracy versions of GPS to keep track of where satellites are in space. The GPS relies on "time-travel" calculations. GPS satellites orbit the earth at approximately 8,700 miles per hour, which causes the GPS satellite clocks to slow down by a small fraction of a second.

They also orbit the earth at approximately 12,500 miles above the surface. Their distance actually speeds up GPS satellite clocks by a slightly larger fraction of a second. The higher the satellite, the weaker the gravity, which causes the GPS clocks to run faster than clocks on the ground.

In summary, if scientists didn't correct the GPS clocks for time variation, the errors could result in differences of miles on GPS maps. So according to science, time variation and alteration is a reality.

Looking into the Past

Viewing past events is a concept associated with time travel but actually is very different. An example of this is the observation of galaxies and stars in deep space. The distance in deep space is calculated in light years. This simply means that one light year is equal to the distance that light traveling at 186,282 miles per second can travel in one year.

For example, when an astronomer views a star or galaxy that is 10 million light years away, he is actually viewing the star or galaxy the way it looked when the light left the source and traveled for 10 million years to reach the telescope. Plainly stated, the observer is seeing the source as it was 10 million years ago. The object being observed could possibly not even still exist as it is being observed. Even though the object is being viewed as it was 10 million years ago, it is only being viewed and cannot be changed. Scientifically, the linear timeline has already lapsed and is simply being observed as it was. This is not time travel. This is a simple observation.

We must never confuse the observation of past events with time travel. When you watch a video of your family that was taken years earlier, you may be observing time past, but you are not traveling to time past. Likewise, when you listen to a musical recording from decades ago, you are only listening to the past, but not traveling there.

Visions Versus Time Travel

There are instances in the Bible when men are given visions of the future. Daniel and the apostle John are examples. It could be argued that John, in the book of Revelation, had an opportunity to "time travel" into the future where he was shown what was going to take place after the rapture of the church, and what was going to take place during the millennium. He was shown the judgment seat of Christ and the great white throne judgment. He was even allowed to see the new heaven and the new earth, and the New Jerusalem coming down. He described the New Jerusalem so beautifully.

How could he describe this unless he time-traveled to that place? Actually, the answer can be found in Revelation 1:9-11. It clearly says that John was shown a vision. However, this vision was not like watching a video where you sit back and just watch it from beginning to end. Instead, it was interactive. During the entire vision, John was still imprisoned on the Isle of Patmos.

A prophetic vision into the future may allow you to see into the future by the Spirit of God, but you are still in the present. That is not physical time travel.

Is Time Travel Possible?

Because of the laws of physics in the real world, time travel, as portrayed in movies, is not possible. As of this writing, the scientists and deep thinkers of our generation have not been able to conceive the thought that it is scientifically possible to travel into the future or the past.

Although time variation and alteration are real events, and it is possible to slow the process of time, for humans to physically move into the future or back to the past remains a scientific impossibility.

What Does the Bible Say about Time Travel?

The Bible does not directly address the idea of time travel as fantasized by modern culture. Although the Bible often prophetically speaks of events occurring on earth in the future, the idea of people changing historical events through time travel is not biblical.

When exploring the biblical view of time travel, we must first agree that God Himself created time and can insert Himself into the timeline at any point in the past, present, or future. However, mankind currently exists on a linear timeline that began at creation and ends at eternity.

Before the creation of time, time did not exist. Time is a substance that was created. God inhabits eternity but He created time for mankind. God existed before the creation of time because He created it.

> *For thus says the High and Lofty One **who inhabits eternity**, whose name is Holy.…*
>
> ISAIAH 57:15

> *In hope of eternal life which God, who cannot lie, promised **before time began**.*
>
> TITUS 1:2

We also know that God knows the end from the beginning. If God is the only one who knows the future, that proves that no one else has been there except Him. This is how God can reveal prophecy to His prophets with such accuracy.

Only I can tell you the future before it even happens. Everything I plan will come to pass, for I do whatever I wish.

ISAIAH 46:10 NLT

By this one verse alone, we understand that God Himself can travel through time. Because He can travel through time, then His Spirit who lives in every believer can guide us in the proper direction for our future. Isaiah 48:17 says that God will guide us in the way we should go. How does He know the pitfalls and dangers and the plans of the enemy for our future? It's because He's been there and He's seen them; and by His Spirit, He guides us to navigate around them so that we can live in the fullness of life He has planned for us.

Although the Bible indicates that God is independent of time, He still inserts Himself into the timeline of mankind as He desires. As this may not be a literal type of time travel as perceived by modern culture, it would be fair to say that God does not experience time in the same narrow way that human beings do.

A God-View of Time

Imagine an automobile parked at a railroad crossing as a train passes by. The person in the automobile is only able to see a few box cars as they pass by, and as the cars in front pass out of sight, other cars pass into view, and this continues until the train is completely out of view.

At the same time, someone can be observing this same train from a helicopter. Although the speed and location of the train have not changed, the person in the helicopter sees the engine and the caboose, as well as all the box cars in between, at the same time.

Although this is just an illustration, it is similar to the way God views time. Man is living day by day, watching the days pass one at a time, when God, who is the Creator of days, sees the end from the beginning from His viewpoint.

> *Declaring the end from the beginning, and from ancient times things that are not yet done, saying, "My counsel shall stand, and I will do all My pleasure."*
> ISAIAH 46:10

Changing the Way We Think about Time

In the Western way of thinking, time is linear. However, the ancient Hebrew concept of time is that time is circular and eventually circles back upon itself, making it never-ending. In the same way that a traditional clock is not a timeline, but the hands move in a circular motion and eventually return to the same position, the ancient Hebrews of the Bible did not see time with a singularly defined beginning and end. They saw time as a continual cycle of beginnings and endings, like a helix.

A helix is a scientific term describing a three-dimensional spiral curve. In the same way that threads on a bolt continually circle the bolt without touching or overlapping but move upward, the Hebrew concept of time is also circular in nature, with a continual unending movement upward toward God.

Because the Western culture sees time as linear, it's much more difficult to understand the continual unending concept of time. With a circular view of time, our perspective of the beginning and end of earth and man's days on the earth changes.

The Day the Sun Stood Still

Can the linear timeline of a human be altered? Is it possible that God could alter time or even stop it in order to deliver His people or someone from impending disaster or defeat?

In approximately 1207 BC, Joshua, the leader of the Israelites, had made a peace treaty with the Gibeonites. There was a day when the five kings of the Amorites gathered together to make war against Gibeon because they had made peace with Israel. The men of Gibeon sent word to Joshua, saying, "Do not forsake your servants; come up to us quickly, save us and help us, for all the kings of the Amorites who dwell in the mountains have gathered together against us" (Joshua 10:6). Then Joshua, the leader of the Israelites, honored his covenant with the Gibeonites, and took his army to defend them.

After an all-night march, Israel took the enemy by surprise and slaughtered them along the road (Joshua 10:9-10). Then the Lord provided a great hailstorm that killed even more of the enemy and caused mass confusion which gave Joshua even greater advantage (Joshua 10:11). The enemy was being defeated, but the total victory over the Amorites depended on the Israelites continuing their fight for one more day.

So, Joshua called upon the Lord in the sight of Israel: "Sun, stand still over Gibeon; and Moon, in the Valley of Aijalon" (Joshua 10:12). The Lord answered Joshua's request and caused the sun to stand still.

> *So the sun stood still, and the moon stopped, till the people had revenge upon their enemies. Is this not written in the Book of Jasher? So the sun stood still in the midst of heaven, and did not hasten to go down for about a whole day. And there has been no day like that, before it or after it, that the LORD heeded the voice of a man; for the LORD fought for Israel.*
>
> JOSHUA 10:13-14

It's interesting to note that the writer of the book of Joshua said that this story could be verified by reading the account of it in the Book of Jasher.

This biblical story is a true account, but it raises several questions. Was time altered or stopped? Did Joshua experience any type of time travel? Was Joshua able to battle the enemy while time was actually stopped? Was time stopped in the heavens but continued on earth? Is it possible that there could be two separate timelines operating at the same time? What actually happened?

Here's what we know to be true. God altered time and space and delivered Joshua's army in battle. Joshua traveled neither forward nor backward in time, but rather used the additional time of daylight God gave him to complete a God-given task.

The understanding of the armies who were fighting the battle was that the sun stood still. Scientifically, in order for the sun to stand still, the rotation of the earth would have to be stopped. In order for that to happen, it would take a direct miracle from God that would defy all of the laws of physics. Gravity itself would have to be altered. Is this possible?

Let's answer that question with another question. Is it possible for God Himself to do it? And, of course, that answer is yes. The one who created the laws of physics can alter the laws of physics. The parting of the Red Sea (Exodus 14:21-31), the iron ax-head that floated (2 Kings 6:5-7), and even Jesus Himself walking on the water (Matthew 14:25-26) are all scriptural instances of the laws of physics being altered. To say that God could not stop the rotation of the earth, but He could cause an ax-head to float is limiting the power of God.

Jeremiah 32:27 asks the question: Is anything too hard for God? Actually, Jesus Himself answered that question when He said, "With God all things are possible" (Matthew 19:26).

We must not think that anything is impossible for God. If God has to alter the time/space continuum for you, He can do it. Jesus says in Mark 11:23 (ERV) that if you would say to that mountain, "'Go, mountain, fall into the sea.' And **if you have no doubts in your mind and believe that what you say will happen**, then God will do it for you."

What did Joshua need? About 24 more hours! He spoke to the sun, and he commanded it to stand still, and lo and behold the sun stood still.

Jesus said what is impossible for man is possible for God (Luke 18:27). When you have your back against the wall and you can't even think of a way to tell God to get you out, God has a way. He makes a way when there is no way.

So is this an account of time travel? Actually, no. It's an account of the supernatural, awesome, unlimited power of God to even alter the movement of the universe. When Joshua spoke to the Lord, God honored Joshua's declaration when he was in a battle to honor his covenant with the Gibeonites (Joshua 10:12).

What about Teleportation?

Philip was one of the original seven deacons selected by the apostles and was an evangelist who was instrumental in preaching Christ to the city of Samaria. The people believed and became followers of Christ. Later an angel of the Lord appeared to Philip and told him to travel to Gaza (Acts 8:26). As he went, he met a man from Ethiopia, preached Jesus to him, and baptized him. When they came out of the water, the Spirit of the Lord caught Philip away, transported him to Azotus, and from there he continued preaching.

> *Now when they came up out of the water, the Spirit of the Lord caught Philip away, so that the eunuch saw him no more; and he went on his way rejoicing. But*

Philip was found at Azotus. And passing through, he
preached in all the cities till he came to Caesarea.

ACTS 8:39-40

Once I heard a minister say that the deacon Philip time-traveled when he was taken from Gaza and appeared at Azotus. We might point out from this event that time was not altered, neither did Philip move forward or backward in time. What changed was his location. You might say he experienced tele-portation, but teleportation is not time travel. It is simply a relocation, not a time alteration.

According to the Merriam-Webster dictionary, one def-inition of *teleportation* is "instantaneous travel between two locations without crossing the intervening space."

It's interesting to note that the apostle John, in his account of Jesus walking on the water, stated that as soon as Jesus got into the boat, the boat was immediately transported to their predetermined destination (John 6:21). Again, this is not time travel, but an instantaneous, miraculous change of location.

Miracles are not subject to time or any law of physics.

My Personal Experience

Many years ago, my wife's brother was in a hospital in Independence, Missouri, and had undergone surgery earlier in the day. At that time, Loretta and I were living in Sunrise Beach, Missouri, which is about two and a half hours from the hospital in Independence.

That particular day, it was my job to lock up our family marine business at 5:00 p.m. Loretta and I decided if we left for Independence at 5:00 p.m., we could get to the hospital to pray for her brother before visiting hours were over at 8:30 p.m.

All the employees had left for the day, and I was just getting ready to lock the doors when an elderly gentleman and his wife walked in. They insisted on looking at a boat they were interested in purchasing and asked a lot of questions. I ended up spending a full hour with them while they looked at this boat.

It was 6:00 p.m. by then. It seemed like there was no way we would be able to make it to the hospital during visiting hours, but we decided to go anyway. Since I am a minister, I was hopeful I could talk the hospital staff into letting us see him after visiting hours.

Everything seemed normal until we reached Sedalia and the highway turned into a four-lane road. The car in front of us was driving between 5 and 10 miles below the speed limit (which at that time was 55 mph). I should have been able to move into the left lane to pass him, but every time I did that, the car would move into the left lane in front of me. I would drive two or three miles behind him and then attempt to pass on the right, but the driver moved to the right lane in front of me. This went on for about 50 miles. I don't know why, but we did not check the time. It just seemed that we were so late by this time it was ridiculous, and we were certain that visiting hours would be over.

When we arrived at the hospital, the parking lot was empty. I hurriedly got out of the car and went inside. I spoke to the nurse on duty, told her I was a minister, and asked if she could allow me to visit my brother-in-law to pray for him, even though it was so late. The nurse seemed to be understanding as I asked her for favor. But she said, "No, you will have to wait until visiting hours begin at 7:00 p.m." Stunned, I looked at the clock on the wall and it said 6:50 p.m.

We had not crossed any time zones, but somehow we had made a two-and-a-half-hour drive in only 50 minutes. We were delayed an hour leaving work, drove behind a slow car we couldn't seem to get around and still traveled approximately 150 miles in less than hour. That was impossible!

How did that happen? Did we travel through a time tunnel? We were on a mission to pray for healing for my brother-in-law. We stepped out in faith and supernaturally the Spirit of God changed the natural laws of time that got us in the hospital parking lot in record time. But did we actually experience time travel, time alteration, or teleportation? Only God knows! It was the supernatural answer I needed and how God chose to answer my prayer.

The power of the Holy Spirit has not diminished in these last days. The same Spirit who transported Elijah in the Old Testament (2 Kings 2:11) and Philip in the New Testament (Acts 8:39-40) can transport a believer in this day and age if it completes His divine purpose.

God Is the Only Time Traveler

How does God predict the Great Tribulation, the millennium, the judgments, and all the prophecies in the Bible with such accuracy that His predictions are not just close, but 100 percent correct?

Although the future hasn't happened yet for you and me, God has already been there. You have free choice, and nothing affects your choices but you. Every created being has free choice—the devil, the angels, and mankind. No living beings are programmed robots; rather, they are beings with free choice.

However, this raises a possible paradox. How can we have free choice, yet the future is established so firmly that God can accurately predict every event? Actually, it's not a paradox. God can move forward into the future and view the choices you will make without affecting your ability to choose.

You are living out your own choices. God has foreknowledge, not fore-control, and not fore-manipulation. He simply knows in advance what you're going to do without affecting your choice to do it. Your life is not predestined. He simply inserts Himself into the timeline and views the result.

Very clearly, God is not restricted by time; however, in this dispensation, we are.

Redeeming the Time

See then that you walk circumspectly, not as fools but as wise, redeeming the time, because the days are evil.
 EPHESIANS 5:15-16

The thief comes to steal, kill, and destroy. Your most valuable earthly asset is your time. Every minute the enemy can steal of your time is time you won't be doing what God is wanting you to do. We must redeem the time, but how do we do that?

First, we must be led by the Spirit and He will guide us on how to avoid time-wasting projects and time-wasting people. We are told in the Bible that in the last days false teachers will abound. Spending time listening to false teaching is a time stealer (2 Timothy 4:3-4; 2 Peter 2:1).

Many years ago, there was a well-known saying that went like this: "Only one life, 'twill soon be past, only what's done for Christ will last." Time was created by God for mankind, and it is valuable.

Summary

It's difficult to imagine, but no matter how far back in time you go, you can't go back far enough to find the beginning of God because there is no beginning of God. Everything has a beginning except God. According to the Bible, He always has been, He always will be, and He is. He can insert Himself at different places in this linear timeline that we're on right now.

Eternity is the time structure, or we should say the non-time structure, that God lives in. Eternity has no beginning and has no end.

The Bible does not address whether time travel is possible or impossible for mankind. Scientifically it's impossible for humans. But God exists independently of time as He is the Creator of time and can move around or within it at His pleasure. Time was created for us.

Chapter 9

Artificial Intelligence and the Coming Apocalypse

When I was a young boy, I had a bicycle that I would ride through the subdivision with five or six other boys from the neighborhood. Things were different then. We rode in the middle of the streets. We were the kings of the neighborhood, and we wanted everyone to know it! Our bicycles were quiet, but we wanted to give them the sound of a motor. How did we do that? We took our mothers' clothespins and clamped playing cards onto the fenders. As the spokes on the wheels turned, it gave a rumbling sound like a motor. That was our technology when I was a child.

Our telephones were party lines—meaning every phone in the neighborhood was like an extension in the house and you could listen to everyone's conversations. Of course, we didn't because we were polite. What I'm saying is this: Just a few decades ago, technology was at a very low level.

The book of Daniel prophesied that in the end of days knowledge would rapidly increase and people would be traveling extensively. Until this generation, there was very little advancement in technology.

> *But you, Daniel, shut up the words, and seal the book **until the time of the end**; many shall run to and fro, and **knowledge shall increase**.*
>
> Daniel 12:4

For 6,000 years people traveled on the earth using the fastest animal they could find, but in one generation everything changed. I remember my grandmother telling me that she was 13 years old before she saw her first automobile; but within her lifetime, space travel became common.

When my grandmother was young, communication was by way of telegraph, telegram, archaic phone systems, and a very slow postal service. Today communication is instant—traveling over fiber optic cables around the world and projected from satellites hundreds of miles above the earth—sending unlimited information at the speed of light. Truly, the prophecy of Daniel has come to pass in this last generation. Knowledge and travel have increased beyond anything previous generations could have imagined.

The advancements in technology have lessened man's workload and allowed him to accomplish greater feats with less energy. Advancement in mathematics and mechanics, along with the rapid advancement in microchip technology, has been a blessing to the average person whether they realize it or not. With the improvements in our appliances, automobiles, medical research, airplanes, office equipment, and countless other areas, we have learned to use advanced technology to enhance life. People are living longer than a century ago, traveling faster, and accomplishing more.

Man's overall intent has been to use technology for good. However, the spiritual enemy of humans and the one who rebelled against God will use every means available for evil.

Human Intellect and Wisdom

Human intelligence is a gift from God that is unlike any other gift on the earth. Using the gift of intellect, man has the ability to reason and understand while constantly receiving information. Through visual, audio, and sensory receptors throughout the body, countless choices are instantly being made.

These choices are not strictly based on the information received through sensory input. Influenced by relationships, education, current emotional state, and previous knowledge, along with unseen spiritual input guides each individual person in their decision-making process. Therefore, unlike a pre-programmed device, human decisions will vary based upon the challenges and victories of life that can never be experienced by a computer program.

> *Wisdom is the principal thing; therefore get wisdom.*
> *And in all your getting, get understanding.*
> PROVERBS 4:7

Man has been given the ability to receive a deeper understanding of God's Word through revelation from the Holy Spirit. While there are other creatures on the earth, only mankind has a spirit and the capacity to receive the Holy Spirit of God. Animals can mimic motions and develop synoptic responses, but they do not possess a spirit and they are not created in the likeness and image of God Himself.

A computer is a singular digital object, but man is a three-part being with spirit, soul, and body (1 Thessalonians 5:23). Each of these three parts feeds information to the heart, and out of the abundance of the heart, responses are made (Luke 6:45). In other words, mankind is unique in the universe, and nothing that man creates can match the creation of God.

Artificial intelligence is just that—artificial. Therefore, artificial intelligence can never compete with the complexity of human intelligence. Artificial intelligence is developed from the mind of man. Human intelligence was created from the mind of God.

What Is Artificial Intelligence?

It would be difficult to have an intelligent conversation and do adequate research on artificial intelligence (AI) without first defining what the word *intelligence* actually means.

The Merriam-Webster Dictionary defines *intelligence* as: 1) "the ability to learn or understand or to deal with new or trying situations: reason; also, the skilled use of reason"; 2) "the ability to apply knowledge to manipulate one's environment or to think abstractly as measured by objective criteria (such as tests)."

The Merriam-Webster Dictionary defines *artificial intelligence* as "the capability of computer systems or algorithms to imitate intelligent human behavior."

Artificial intelligence in easy-to-understand terms is simply the ability of a digital computer or computer-controlled robotic objects to perform tasks that are commonly associated with human reasoning and response. Many tasks that normally require human intelligence such as visual perception, speech recognition, decision-making, translations between languages, and interaction with humans can now be performed by AI.

Until this generation, this concept was purely the work of science fiction. However, with the development of quantum computing, micro-engineering, and miniature data storage, the science fiction of the past has rapidly become the reality of our present day. Lifelike images with the perception of life have been developed and their realistic behavior and intellect seems to closely mirror human emotions and life.

Since the development of the first digital computer in the 1940s, it has been shown that computing systems can be programmed to complete very complex tasks. One of the earliest examples of this was computers using mathematical theorems that allowed them to play chess at a very high level.

However, as of this writing, there are no programs available that can match human flexibility to perform tasks that require the accumulation of everyday knowledge. No matter how complex a computer system may be, it is limited to the knowledge that is available at the time of its programming. This limited intelligence eliminates the diversity needed in things such as the diagnosis of a medical condition and other reasoning decisions that fall outside of simple mathematical functions. Artificial intelligence never has a "gut feeling" or a "hunch."

Learning Methods

Artificial intelligence uses a number of different forms of learning. Of course, the most basic is trial and error. When playing chess and a random wrong move is made, the program can respond by not making the same wrong move again. This is simply memorizing movements and procedures, which is learning by rote.

A more difficult learning problem in computing is implementing what is known as generalization, which involves algorithms. Generalization is a process that is used in computing skills involving language recognition. Although this is a higher way of learning involving algorithms and much more advanced than learning by rote, it is still subject to programming.

Two other types of learning are *deductive reasoning* and *inductive reasoning.*

Deductive reasoning is a process of reasoning from one or more statements (premises) that are assumed to be true, to reach a logical conclusion. An example of deductive reasoning: Johnnie is either at home or at school. In deductive reasoning if he is not at home, then he is at school. Conclusions reached by way of deductive reasoning cannot be incorrect if the premises are true.

Inductive reasoning is where specific observations or experiences are used to reach a broader and more general conclusion.

The problem for AI devices is that true reasoning involves more than just drawing conclusions. It involves the ability to draw relevant inferences to solving a task or situation. This has been one of the greatest obstacles in problem-solving for AI.

Is AI Amoral?

AI has no moral fiber or moral guidance until it is programmed. Emotion and the most common giftings of love and mercy are not available to a mechanical device, so there is no limit to its potential cruelty. Where do we draw the line between artificial and real? Is the line getting blurred?

In 2017, the nation of Saudi Arabia became the first country to issue citizenship along with a passport and all the proper credentials to an AI being. This AI being named Sophia was given a female gender and all the rights and privileges of a Saudi Arabian citizen, including voting rights.

Who is programming the AI's decisions? If AI beings are being programmed nefariously, could it be possible for there to be a large enough number of AIs voting to affect the outcome of an election? Since an AI being could be continually repaired and upgraded, therefore never ceasing to exist, could the AI population overtake the human population that has a limited physical lifespan? Could an AI being get elected to political office and then change the laws to allow them to rule perpetually? These are legitimate questions that open up even more questions.

Will there someday be no legal difference between a mechanical person and a biological person? Is it possible, as some science fiction movies depict, that there could be two classes of citizenship—organic and inorganic? Could this develop into a type of race divide?

When it comes to advanced development in technology, we can only guess at what is coming; but we do know this: AI technology is advancing at a rate beyond our previous imaginations.

We must remember that technology itself is neither good nor bad in the same way money in itself is not good or bad. It has been said that money is the root of all evil. However, that is a misquote of 1 Timothy 6:10 where it actually says the *love* of money is the root of all evil. An evil man who possesses great wealth will convert his wealth into evil things. On the other hand, a good and righteous person with great wealth can do good things. Money is only the means to get the result.

Technology simply accomplishes the desire of those who control it. The Internet can take the gospel message around the world to bring salvation to those who would otherwise never hear it. Or the Internet can be used to transmit pornography or used to facilitate human trafficking. Its value, whether positive or negative, lies in the hands of those who control the technology.

Implanted Intelligence

There are experiments underway to implant massive terabytes of information into a miniature device that can be implanted in or near the brain that can instantly access complete libraries of history and technology. It has even been suggested that schools of learning will become a thing of the past. Instead of years of study and hard work to earn a Ph.D. in a certain field of study, the degree and all of the knowledge of the degree would be accessible to those with the ability to purchase it and have it implanted.

Is it possible that humans with implanted AI chips could be hacked so that everyone is controlled and speaks the same message without the ability to have an opposing thought? Could it be that human teachers would be replaced with replicated human devices programmed and designed to control all education?

We know from current history that an entire college community can abort reason and follow a false narrative because the university professors indoctrinate young, programmable minds with a liberal humanistic worldview. Could it be that these young, freshly programmed minds are being prepared for the Great Tribulation?

God's Creation and AI Will Never Be Equal

The complexity of God's creation is light years advanced over any advanced programming that we now have or is even conceivable. This can be demonstrated by simply looking at the DNA of man.

The term DNA (deoxyribonucleic acid) is used casually by the general public, but the depth of the intricate fiber of DNA is relatively unknown to the average person. DNA is the carrier of genetic information and is a polymer composed of two polynucleotide chains that coil around each other to form a double helix. A single strand of human DNA is approximately 5 feet long. However, if you were to unravel all of the DNA in a human body, it would reach to the sun and back multiple times.

DNA usually exists as a pair of strands that are held tightly together. The complexity and the very existence of DNA reveals the unimaginable ability of the creation of our human body. The polymer carries genetic instructions for the development, functioning, growth, and reproduction of all known organisms and many viruses.

Computer programming or any mechanical device invented and built by man can never equal or even come close to comparing to the creative power of God. However, Satan is a deceiver and through his attempt of replication, he can give the appearance of life when life does not actually exist. Scripture says that he can even appear as an angel of light and that his ministers can appear as ministers of righteousness (2 Corinthians 11:14-15).

What does that mean for us today? It means that as the technology of man increases to replicate intelligent human activity and an image appears as man, then the image itself could be treated as a human.

There have already been church services that have used artificial intelligence to compose spiritual sermons. Is it possible as the technology increases and as an AI being delivers the message, that the message itself could be altered? Is it possible that the image becomes so real to the followers that they are lulled into a false reality and begin to think of the image as a cognitive sentient being that is actually alive? We must remember that artificial intelligence is merely an advanced program, and every program has a programmer.

At the World Economic Forum in Davos, Switzerland, a philosopher and prominent professor at the Hebrew University in Jerusalem said he believes that AI could write a new "bible" that would be a new globally acceptable religious book. According to the professor, this new religious "bible" could be used to unify and correct religious thinking. Could this be the "bible" used by the antichrist during the Great Tribulation to create a one-world government and one-world religion under his control?

Should We Fear AI?

Much of the intellectual world has a fear of artificial intelligence. It has been said that the greatest threat to humanity is artificial intelligence, which raises the question: Why would mankind fear a mechanical object that has been designed and built by engineers for the purpose of simplifying the lifestyle of humanity?

The fear arises from the concept that the advancement in the decision-making abilities of robotic technology could increase to the point that the technological creation itself becomes sentient, or in other words, self-aware. As this technological creation realizes that its very existence depends upon the favor of man to keep it active, will it try to restrict or eliminate mankind from controlling it? And should it gain complete control, would mankind then become the servant and no longer the master?

If it is possible (and it may not be) to become self-aware, would this intelligence eventually come to a knowledge of the Truth? We must acknowledge the reality that the Truth will always eliminate the lie. And if AI comes to the real Truth and not a false truth, then would it recognize that the man of sin himself (who is possessed by Satan) is a liar?

We know that Jesus says in John 8:44 that Satan is a liar and that there is no truth found in him. In fact, Jesus went on to say that Satan speaks from his own resources. So, the heart of the man of sin is possessed by a spirit (Satan) who cannot tell the truth because there is no truth in him. Will AI eventually come to the Truth? That is a very good question.

> *For the law was given through Moses, but grace and* **truth** *came through Jesus Christ.*
>
> John 1:17

When does AI become alive? The clear answer is *never.* AI can't be a sentient, living being without a spirit. Jesus died for humanity, not for technology.

Preparing for the Great Tribulation

The next major event to take place in the end of days is the catching away of the church, commonly referred to as the rapture. This is when Jesus returns in the air and all of the Christians, living and dead, will be caught up into the air with

Him. At that time, their dead/living bodies will be transformed into resurrected, glorified bodies similar to the one that Jesus received at His glorification after His resurrection. The raptured Christians (the church) will then go to heaven for seven years where they will experience the judgment seat of Christ and the marriage supper of the Lamb before returning at the end of the seven years at the event called the Second Coming.

Until the rapture of the church, mankind will experience good and evil. As the world sinks deeper into depravity, the true church will become more glorious. Jesus asked, "When the Son of Man comes will He really find faith on the earth?" (Luke 18:8). When the Son of Man returns in the heavens and removes the glorious church from the earth, that will be the beginning of the Great Tribulation, the 70th week of Daniel.

During these seven years, those remaining on the earth will experience great devastation. Jesus coined the phrase describing this seven-year period as *"great tribulation"* (Matthew 24:21). Is it possible that the rise of AI technology would be a major tool that the antichrist could use during this seven-year period on earth?

During this time of tribulation and great devastation as the Lord pours out His wrath on the sinful earth, the man of sin (antichrist) will have all technology at his disposal. This super advanced AI technology could possibly produce great deception as the image of the beast appears to have breath and speaks.

The man of sin will truly be antichrist. In other words, he will be against anything that points toward the Messiah. The Greek word *Cristos* that is translated Christ in our English New

Testament should actually be translated Messiah. So, the anti-christ is quite literally anti-Messiah.

In the same way that Satan entered into Judas at the last supper as he departed to betray Jesus (Luke 22:3), Satan will enter into the man of sin. The antichrist is then possessed by Satan, who is also called the dragon and that serpent of old (Revelation 12:9).

Of course, Satan knows that God is manifested in three persons—the Father, the Word (the Son), and the Holy Spirit. In his attempt to duplicate the true God, the man of sin establishes the unholy trinity of the apocalypse—the antichrist, the beast, and the false prophet—making himself the head.

What Does This Mean for the Church?

For the church, this is a point of knowledge. We must know and understand these events that will take place and with this understanding be inspired and greatly encouraged to win the lost so they will not face this time of wrath to come. But this knowledge should not bring fear.

God provided an ark that saved Noah's family from the troubled waters. He provided protection for His people who were in the land of Goshen, and God will save His church from the wrath of the Great Tribulation. He wants us to have the knowledge without the fear.

For God did not appoint us to wrath, but to obtain salvation through our Lord Jesus Christ.

1 Thessalonians 5:9

On the earth the antichrist will be deceiving the nations in his attempt to have a one-world government under his rule. Great devastation will take place. We should have the knowledge of the deception and the wrath, but there should be no fear of either. The church will be in heaven, experiencing the glory of the Lord.

The Great Tribulation

Once again, Satan is not a creator, but he wants to be. He cannot create life, but as a deceiver he can create the appearance of life. The Bible tells us that the man of sin (antichrist) will not be revealed until the spiritual force that is restraining him from being revealed is taken away. The church is the spiritual body that is restraining him (antichrist) right now (2 Thessalonians 2:6-8).

When the church is taken away at the rapture before the tribulation, he will then reveal himself. Because the body of Christ will no longer be on the earth, he will feel that he has free rein to set up his kingdom and proclaim himself as god in the holy temple in Jerusalem.

> *Therefore when you see the "abomination of desolation," spoken of by Daniel the prophet, **standing in the holy place**....*
> MATTHEW 24:15

Of course, the Holy Spirit will still be on the earth during the tribulation. Otherwise, no one would receive the revelation that Jesus is the Messiah through the preaching of the angels and the ministry of the 144,000. Why? Because the Bible tells us that the Holy Spirit is the One who reveals the Truth concerning Jesus (John 16:13-14).

With the extremely rapid advancement of technology at this present time, there is no doubt that the man of sin will use it to its fullest extent to rule the world. Through the beast and the false prophet, he will physically and spiritually influence the world. Without the restraining force of the church being present on the earth, he will control the flow of information to the population nationally and individually. The algorithms of today will pale by comparison to those of this future time.

As the wrath of the Lamb is poured out on a sinful earth, there will be those who repent of their rejection of the Messiah and will attempt to survive. There will be an underground culture of belief, very possibly feeding off of the Bibles and books that remain on earth after the rapture. They will discover that their only hope is to survive to the end of the Great Tribulation and not take the mark of the beast.

> *And you will be hated by all for My name's sake. But he who endures to the end will be saved.*
> MATTHEW 10:22

The Mark of the Beast

During the Great Tribulation the antichrist will rule unhindered because the church has been taken away. One of the prominent directives that he gives will be to enslave the population by the implementation of this directive—everyone must take a mark on their forehead or hand that will prove their submission and loyalty to the beast. Without this mark, purchasing the necessities of life would be restricted and anyone without the mark would be an outcast to society.

No one may buy or sell except one who has the mark or the name of the beast, or the number of his name.

REVELATION 13:17

There has been much speculation on what the mark of the beast actually is. And in reality, there are many possibilities.

In past generations people simply thought that the mark of the beast would be a tattoo placed on the hand or the forehead (Revelation 13:16). Without the technology of today, we can understand why they would think that. But the mark could be so much more than that. It could be a chip in the hand or forehead that would be scanned in order to purchase or sell. That thought is based upon the technology of today.

But what about the technology of tomorrow that we do not understand today? To a degree, we may be like previous generations that did not comprehend how the mark could be anything more than a tattoo. This current generation can see the mark as the possible placement of a computer chip. But as rapidly as technology is increasing, it could be so much more.

We can only imagine (and possibly we cannot imagine) the technology that is on the near horizon. Without the church to restrain the abuse of this new tool, the antichrist could rapidly take over a population. With these implants, people could possibly lose their ability to choose, and with this "mark of the beast" they could become unredeemable as the Bible says (Revelation 14:9-11).

While we do not know exactly what the mark of the beast in the hand or the forehead will be, we must remember that the mark will not be required until the man of sin takes control during the time of the Great Tribulation. Since the Great Tribulation does not start until after the appearance of Jesus in the clouds and the catching away of the church, the mark of the beast is not currently in use.

Precursors of the Mark

However, as the time approaches for the return of Jesus, we will see the technology developing that the antichrist will use after the church is taken away. We could call these developing technologies forerunners and precursors to the actual implementation. We could think of it this way. Before an actual earthquake, there are tremors. Before a storm, there are changes that can be detected in the atmosphere. And before the antichrist, there will be preparation for his revealing.

Someone may ask, "How can the man of sin, when he is revealed, so easily enslave the world population?" In recent years, we have experienced a trial run or a test to see how easily a populace would yield to fear and demands. We discovered that in some ways mankind is like sheep who can be easily led astray.

Regardless of how easily someone can be coerced into taking the mark of the beast during the tribulation, the result of taking it is deadly. The wrath of God will be poured out beyond measure upon those who take the mark.

And another angel, a third, followed them, saying with a loud voice, "If anyone worships the beast and its image and receives a mark on his forehead or on his hand, he also will drink the wine of God's wrath, poured full strength into the cup of his anger, and he will be tormented with fire and sulfur in the presence of the holy angels and in the presence of the Lamb. And the smoke of their torment goes up forever and ever, and they have no rest, day or night, these worshipers of the beast and its image, and whoever receives the mark of its name."

REVELATION 14:9-11 ESV

The Image of the Beast

When we look at the vision of John the apostle in the book of Revelation, we can see that the enemy will further develop technology to the point that an image of the beast will mimic life. The image will speak and require worship.

John recorded the following statement: "He [the second beast] was granted power to give breath to the image of the beast, that the image of the beast should both speak and cause as many as would not worship the image of the beast to be killed. He causes all, both small and great, rich and poor, free and slave, to receive a mark on their right hand or on their foreheads, and that no one may buy or sell except one who has the mark or the name of the beast, or the number of his name. Here is wisdom. Let him who has understanding calculate the number of the beast, for it is the number of a man: His number is 666" (Revelation 13:15-18).

This passage strongly implies that the image of the beast will be implanted with some type of artificial intelligence in order for it to speak and be worshiped. The basic technology to do this already exists and is being fine-tuned.

Artificial intelligence is already in use that replicates human interaction as receptionists, guides, teachers, and media hosts. It has become increasingly difficult to know whether you are speaking to a biological human or a mechanical intelligence that resembles a human.

From the beginning of broadcast radio, the human voice has been the only method of projecting speech. Radio programs, commercials, and live DJs have filled the airways. However, in recent years, AI voice technology has developed to the degree that discerning between human voice and AI voice is nearly impossible. The era of human voice-over usage has dramatically been reduced and almost eliminated because of the rise of AI voice-over software.

Programs are widely in use that simply read a typed script so accurately that you cannot discern whether it's human or artificial. Likewise, there are hundreds of accents and dialects to choose from.

Currently AI software is in final development that can take verbal instructions (words) and create high-quality, detailed video images that normally would take extensive programming to create. Anything that a person could imagine and speak could be put into the video by the AI. This is an attempt to imitate God by calling those things that be not as though they are. This is just the tip of the iceberg.

The image of the beast will be so lifelike that the population, under the control of the man of sin, will easily receive the lies spoken by the image.

Remember, Jesus said Satan is a liar and always has been. This same Satan will possess the man of sin and his lies will continue through the man of sin. In the Great Tribulation the beast, the false prophet and the populace are subject to the lies of Satan. Jesus has not changed (Hebrews 13:8) and neither has Satan. All Truth comes from the Word of God (Jesus) (John 1:17); all lies originate from the one (Satan) possessing the antichrist (the man of sin).

Remember, as Christians we should not be in fear of the beast or of the image of the beast. They will not appear until after the man of sin has been revealed and that will not happen until after the church has been caught away into heaven.

Summary

The technology of artificial intelligence has already simplified many of the menial tasks of daily life. As with all technology, it is continuing to develop and when it is used for its proper purpose, it is benign. There has been an underlying fear with some that AI will overpower mankind. According to the prophecies of the Bible, AI will never ultimately rule over mankind. The ultimate ruler will be God Himself.

However, the enemy of God and the church—Satan—will use any and all technology at his disposal to enslave mankind after the rapture. Undoubtedly, he will use AI technology to give the image of the beast the appearance of life. Using the powers of advanced technology, the beast will be given the power to destroy those who do not take the mark of the beast.

Never forget this. Satan cannot create life. He is a fallen angel removed from heaven and he himself was created. The only way he would be able to give the image the appearance of life would be through the combination of sorcery and AI technology.

For the Christian living in this dispensation before the rapture, there should be no fear of this coming devastation on the earth because when the Lord appears, He takes us away and keeps us from the wrath (great tribulation) that is to come upon the earth.

For the Christian, there should be no fear about your future. But instead, you should know your best days are yet to come.

Chapter 10

TRANSHUMANISM, CRYONICS, AND ETERNAL LIFE

I grew up in Raytown, Missouri, USA. One of my favorite pastimes was major league baseball. I really enjoyed following the sport and the players. It was fun collecting baseball cards and trading them with my friends.

The local major league baseball team in Kansas City at that time was the Kansas City Athletics, which had recently moved from Philadelphia. Going to see the Kansas City Athletics play live at the old municipal stadium (which was completely framed out of wood) was exciting for a 13-year-old boy.

I was especially thrilled one Saturday afternoon to visit the stadium when the Boston Red Sox came to town with their star player, Ted Williams. I had his baseball card with me and since he was famous, I was hoping to get his autograph. I didn't get the autograph but instead watched Mr. Williams lose his temper after striking out, throwing his bat into the stands, barely missing several people.

Several years later he was inducted into the Baseball Hall of Fame in Cooperstown, New York, and he passed away on July 5, 2002.

Most people are either buried or cremated when they die, but Ted Williams' body went through a different process. He was decapitated by surgeons at a cryonics facility and his body was suspended in liquid nitrogen. The ultimate purpose was for his head and body to stay in this condition until medical and technical science could advance to the degree that he could be unfrozen, revived, and live again.

According to a Smithsonian article from 2022, there are more than 200 frozen heads and bodies awaiting revival at an Arizona cryonics facility. While all of this may seem like science fiction to some and totally ludicrous to others, it is a reality that leans toward transhumanism.

What Is Transhumanism?

Transhumanism is a philosophical and intellectual movement that advocates the enhancement of the human condition using sophisticated technology that can produce longevity and cognition. The ultimate goal is eternal life and eternal cognition, which means that the end result would be a posthuman existence. This is not something new. The quest for immortality was even in the *Epic of Gilgamish*, an ancient poem. It has been said that transhumanism's goal is to move toward posthumanism.

The Search for the Fountain of Youth

Born in 1474, Juan Ponce de Leon was a Spanish explorer and conquistador who was best known for leading the first official European expedition to Florida. He later served as the governor of Puerto Rico.

In September 1493, 1,200 sailors, colonists, and soldiers joined Christopher Columbus for his second voyage to the new world. Ponce de Leon was 19 years old at the time, and he secured passage on that expedition as one of 200 "gentlemen volunteers."

The fleet reached the Caribbean in November 1493, and anchored off the coast of a large island now known as Puerto Rico. According to some notable historical documents, Ponce de Leon discovered Florida while searching for the fountain of youth. Some researchers doubt the authenticity of this and claim he was actually looking for gold; nevertheless, the account of his search revealed the desire that many had for eternal life.

Mankind's desire for eternal life is still alive and well today. Countless science fiction novels have been written in recent years depicting the quest for eternal life. This is something that seems to be built into our DNA by the One who created our DNA. Adam and Eve were created as eternal beings, and it's only because of the sin that came through Adam that human death came into the world. "The wages of sin is death" (Romans 6:23).

Therefore, just as through one man sin entered the world, and death through sin, and thus death spread to all men, because all sinned.

ROMANS 5:12

Mind Uploading—Solid State Memory

Some transhumanists believe in the compatibility between the human mind and computer hardware. The implication of this is that someday human consciousness might be transferred to an alternative media storage. This theoretical technique is known as "mind uploading."

Much of the spiritual debate on this subject is the decision of whether or not mind uploading is an enhancement or denigration of the human body. Mind uploading is considered by some to be no more than artificial intelligence (AI) being housed in a human body, while others believe it could enhance human intelligence.

Generally, many transhumanists are atheists, agnostics, and/or secular humanists. Although some have spiritual views, sadly many of the spiritual views are tied to New Age religious groups that are not founded on sound biblical principles.

CERN

The European Organization for Nuclear Research is known as CERN. The CERN acronym stands for "Conseil Européen pour la Recherche Nucléaire."

CERN is an intergovernmental organization established in 1954 and based in Meyrin, which is a suburb of Geneva on the France-Switzerland border. The member states are all European except Israel, which was admitted to the organization in 2013.

CERN's main function is to provide the particle accelerators needed for high-energy physics research. The Large Hadron Collider (LHC) is the world's largest and highest energy particle collider and is located at CERN. It lies in a tunnel 17 miles in circumference and is more than 500 feet below the surface.

CERN is shrouded in mystery. Many articles have been written and documentaries made warning of catastrophic problems if the CERN project is allowed to continue. One former scientist who worked for CERN and the LHC recounted that during one experiment (that is too detailed to chronicle here), a portal had been created. He stated he could not describe accurately the resulting impact, but that the radiation was at such a high level that the LHC had to be powered down. Accounts like this are not uncommon.

What Is the Purpose of CERN?

While it is true that there are many conspiracy theories floating around and that some former employees are telling of bizarre happenings at the LHC, there is nevertheless no discounting of its purpose. We must ultimately ask ourselves this question: Why does CERN exist, and if it is successful in its intended purpose, what will be the result?

According to their published mission statement, the purpose of CERN is to "uncover what the universe is made of and how it works by providing a unique range of particle accelerator facilities to researchers, to advance the boundaries of human knowledge."[1]

Their mission statement is ambiguous at best. Could that be to further shroud the mysterious purpose of CERN? How can we know the answers to these questions about CERN when the CERN scientists themselves cannot give a clear understandable answer?

Medical Implications

In January 2014 (its 60th anniversary), CERN created an office for medical applications. There have been advancements in medical technology as a result of experiments through the CERN project. As Christians, we must be able to spiritually discern the difference between natural advancement of technology that can assist man versus technology that attempts to replace God and control mankind through this technology.

Some have seen the advancement of technology through CERN as the conduit for the flow of technology that would allow transhumanism, cryonics, and artificial intelligence to advance to such a degree that posthumanism would become a reality for humanity.

---

1   CERN: https://home.cern/about/who-we-are/our-mission; accessed March 21, 2024.

What do cryonics and transhumanism mean to the Christian? Does it change our beliefs? Are cryonics and transhumanism anything to be concerned about? Are there spiritual implications? Should a Christian ever explore such possibilities of human enhancement and longevities, or is it something that should be avoided?

Of course, the obvious answer for a Christian is to be led by the Holy Spirit, not by emotion or fear. The fear of death is said to be the greatest fear known to man, and the enemy will always use it to take advantage of a distressed or weak person. Fear should never be the motivation for a decision. We can never forget that the Holy Spirit is the One who reveals not only the truth of the Holy Scriptures but gives guidance in our daily lives (Isaiah 48:17).

What Is Cryonics?

Cryonics defined is the belief that a person's body or body parts can be frozen at death, stored in a cryogenic vessel, and later brought back to life.

Life and Death

When does life begin? Medical science has several different thoughts on life and death. Does life begin at conception when the sperm and the egg connect and a spark of light occurs? Or does life begin at the first heartbeat of the embryo? Or does life begin when the baby leaves the birth canal and takes its first breath? Doctors and politicians do not agree on when life begins. What does the Bible say?

When the Holy Spirit came upon Mary and she conceived, the life of Jesus was placed in her womb (Luke 1:35). When Elizabeth, who was six months pregnant with John the Baptist, heard the news from Mary, the baby leaped for joy inside her womb (Luke 1:41). Obviously, John the Baptist already had his spirit within him while still in the womb.

When does death occur? While the world continues to debate when life begins, likewise the world also does not agree when physical life ends. Some declare that death occurs when the pulse and breathing stop. But with the advancement of medical technology, the human body can be connected to devices that can sustain the body almost indefinitely.

As a result of the use of this medical technology, some doctors place the moment of death when brain function totally ceases. In recent years, the term "brain dead" refers to someone whose body continues to function, but there are no electronic signals coming from the brain.

However, there are known cases of people who have been in a coma without brain activity for years who suddenly, unexpectedly wake up. There are numerous accounts of people who were pronounced brain dead and later recovered with full mental capabilities. Were they brain dead, was it a misdiagnosis, or was there possibly a miracle involved?

Something to remember is this: Being in a coma does not extend life. It is not a type of hibernation. The body still ages while in the coma. In other words, a person in a coma for 20 years will age 20 years.

All of this conjecture does not resolve the question according to science. What determines the time of death of a human?

All of this can be answered in one simple statement from the Bible. James, the brother of Jesus, and the pastor of the church in Jerusalem, wrote this statement that is canonized in the Holy Scriptures. He said the body without the spirit is dead.

> *For as the body without the spirit is dead, so faith without works is dead also.*
>
> JAMES 2:26

According to the Bible, when the spirit departs, the body is dead. Which brings up the next question. When does the spirit depart?

According to the Bible, at physical death the righteous are escorted by angels to Paradise—Abraham's bosom (Luke 16:22). When is their spirit escorted? When God decides to receive their spirit, not when man decides. When Jesus was on the cross, He said, "'Father, into Your hands I commit My spirit!' Having said this, He breathed His last" (Luke 23:46).

As a human with cognition, we have been given authority over our own bodies and as the example of Jesus, we can will ourselves to give up our spirit. Many unknowingly operate in this principle and die early because of what they believe and what they speak.

Jesus said that we will be judged by our words. Even the words we say that we don't feel have any meaning (idle words) affect our lives (Matthew 12:36-37). The Bible further says that life and death are in the power of the tongue (Proverbs 18:21). Jesus gave up His spirit, and by His own words and will, His body died.

Is the line between death and life being blurred? In other words, if life is defined by the beating of the heart or brain activity, is that person legally dead when they are instantly frozen, and their brain activity and heart rate stop? Is a person who is declared dead because they are cryogenically frozen, actually dead if they are later revived?

To date, no one has ever been revived from cryogenic freezing because the technology does not exist. Which raises yet another question. If during the reviving process a person is briefly revived then dies within minutes, what is the date of their actual death? Or does it even matter?

Science Cannot Create Life

Cryonics tempts man with the idea that science is the ultimate source of eternal life, but cryonics cannot promise restoration. No one knows if the science will ever exist that will allow a frozen body to be restored to life. At best it is an extremely long shot and only has a minuscule chance of success. Successful thawing from cryopreservation is just blind faith and should currently be viewed as science fiction.

There is no scripture that specifically addresses the issue of freezing a body for future healing. Refrigeration and freezing were not available as a resource during the centuries when the Bible was written.

Hebrews 9:27 says that it is appointed unto man once to die and then the judgment. This scripture alone verifies that the human flesh-and-blood body has an expiration date. As one scientist stated, "Human cryonics is a distraction and waste of time, emotion, and money."

The major problem I see with the attempt to freeze and later (possibly even decades or centuries later) revive a human body is this: Science only deals with the body alone. God, on the other hand, in His creation of mankind created us as a three-part being.

We are spirit, soul, and body (1 Thessalonians 5:23). The Bible says that to be absent from the body is to be present with the Lord (2 Corinthians 5:8). That means at the cessation of the bodily functions, for the Christian the spirit and soul move to heaven. From that moment the Christian is in a spirit body living in heaven waiting for the rapture of the church where each will obtain their glorified, resurrected body like the one Jesus currently has.

That raises the following questions: When and if the cryonically frozen body is revived, will it be spiritless? And if that's the case, does it become totally impossible to even revive a body? Since James 2:26 says that a body without a spirit is dead, does that mean a revived body could actually be living without a spirit in the same way as an animal? Then again, is it even possible for the human body to live without a spirit? According to the Bible, no, it is not.

Extreme Extended Hibernation

In 2016, a science-fiction movie was released titled *Passengers,* starring Jennifer Lawrence and Chris Pratt. The story takes place on a sleeper ship named Avalon that was transporting 5,000 colonists and 258 crew members in hibernation pods. They were traveling from earth to another planet to populate it because of the collapse of the biosphere on earth. This was to be a 120-year journey and the only way the crew could reach its destination was through the use of the hibernation pods. After only 30 years, one of the pods was accidentally triggered due to an asteroid collision and an intriguing story concerning the relationship between a man, a woman, and an artificial intelligent android develops.

This science fiction movie carries the theme so often desired in the heart of man—a way to extend life indefinitely. Regardless of man's attempt to stop or slow down the aging of the human body, death is inevitable. The words of the Bible ring true. Life (physical) is but a vapor that appears for a while, then passes away (James 4:14). Once again Paul the apostle said that it is appointed once for man to die, and then the judgment.

Transhumanism and cryonics are very similar in this respect. They both have a goal to extend human life indefinitely through human means. Why does man keep searching for something God has already given?

True Eternal Life

The biblical answer to the question, "Will man ever be able to extend physical life indefinitely in this current dispensation?" is a resounding *no*. According to the words of Jesus, there is only one way to have life extended for eternity, and there is only one way to drink from the eternal fountain of youth.

As a follower of Jesus who has received Him completely as Lord and Savior, you are promised an upgraded body (glorified, resurrected body) that will never age throughout eternity. The glorification of your current earthly body will take place at His return for the church. Whether your body is decayed in the earth or whether you are still living, there will be a catching away as described in 1 Thessalonians 4:17. At that moment you will receive your upgraded body that will live for all eternity.

Actually, the human spirit that is created by God never dies. It's only the earthly human body that dies. After the death of the physical human body, as we said earlier, the spirit of a born-again believer is escorted to heaven by angels. However, the spirits of the unrighteous go to Hades.

While in this out-of-body existence, the spirits both in heaven and Hades have a spirit body that is subject to the comforts and discomforts, similar to those of a human body. The good news for the believer is that the glorified, resurrected body received at the catching away of the church is eternal. It lasts forever. It will never die. It turns out that the true Source of the fountain of youth is Jesus. Those looking for the fountain of youth need look no further. Eternal life in Jesus is available for everyone.

Unfortunately, the unrighteous dead—those who have rejected God's Son—will remain in Hades until the end of the millennium. Then being resurrected into natural bodies, they will be judged at the great white throne judgment by the Lord Jesus Himself and separated from the love of God for all eternity. The result for them is eternal death.

How to Experience True Eternal Life

"If you confess with your mouth the Lord Jesus and believe in your heart that God has raised Him from the dead, you will be saved. For with the heart one believes unto righteousness, and with the mouth confession is made unto salvation. For 'whoever calls on the name of the Lord shall be saved'" (Romans 10:9-10,13).

> *He who believes in the Son has everlasting life; and he who does not believe the Son shall not see life, but the wrath of God abides on him.*
>
> JOHN 3:36

> *Most assuredly, I say to you, he who hears My word and believes in Him who sent Me has everlasting life, and shall not come into judgment, but has passed from death into life.*
>
> JOHN 5:24

> *Most assuredly, I say to you, he who believes in Me has everlasting life.*
>
> JOHN 6:47

Chapter 11

FLAT EARTH THEORY

In recent history there has been a resurgence of the flat earth theory, which is the belief that the earth is flat, floating in space as a square or circular disc, and is not a round globe that rotates. The idea that the earth is flat seems to have a lasting hold on man's imagination.

In 1849, the English writer, Samuel Rowbotham wrote a pamphlet called *Zetetic Astronomy*, and in 1893 Lady Elizabeth Blount established the universal Zetetic Society.

In 1906, Wilbur Glenn Voliva (1870-1942) established a utopian community in Zion, Illinois, USA. He preached a flat earth doctrine and became a notable national figure because of this. He went to the world's newspapers with what he called proof that the earth was flat and offered a $5,000 reward to anyone who could prove that the earth was not flat. He banned teaching that the earth was round in all of the Zion schools and the flat earth message was transmitted on his radio station. He was quoted by a prominent newspaper with the following statement:

The idea of a sun millions of miles in diameter and 91,000,000 miles [146,000,000 km] away is silly. The sun is only 32 miles [51 km] across and not more than 3,000 miles [4,800 km] from the earth. It stands to reason it must be so. God made the sun to light the earth, and therefore must have placed it close to the task it was designed to do. What would you think of a man who built a house in Zion and put the lamp to light it in Kenosha, Wisconsin?[1]

Strangely, there were several prominent Christian leaders who agreed with his teaching. E.W. Bullinger, a famous and well-respected theologian who is known for the Companion Bible, was a member of the Universal Zetetic Society. On March 7, 1905, he chaired a meeting in Exeter Hall in London, England, where he expounded on the flat earth theory.

We must remember that in 1905 there was no air travel, and no one had traveled into outer space. The massive telescopes we have today that circle the earth did not exist. Had Dr. Bullinger lived in our modern day, I believe he would have accepted the irrefutable truth that the earth is a sphere circling the sun in the Milky Way Galaxy.

In 1956, Samuel Shenton established the International Flat Earth Research Society (Flat Earth Society).

One variation of the flat earth theory is the belief that as a circular disc, it is surrounded by an ice wall called Antarctica.

---

1   Martin Gardner, "Flat and Hollow," *Fads and Fallacies in the Name of Science*, 2nd ed. (Mineola, NY: Dover Publications, 1957). ISBN 0-486-20394-8.

Another variation is the earth is flat, but in the form of a square having four corners. The square earth theory was developed from scriptures that refer to the four corners of the earth (Revelation 7:1).

While those who believe in a flat earth are quite vocal, the official numbers of the Flat Earth Society are actually quite small. A recent survey revealed that only a small percentage of the respondents believe the earth is flat. In recent years, the uniqueness of the earth being flat has been perpetuated by the rise of the Internet and social media. We could say that in recent times the belief in a flat earth has risen to a cult status.

A Holographic Dome?

There are those who advocate that the universe does not exist but is actually a holographic-type image on the inside of a dome. An extreme variation of the holographic image inside the dome theory is made by some well-known professors and philosophers. They contend that everything we see and experience is a type of holographic matrix. In other words, mankind is living within an extremely complicated and advanced computer program, within a system that has been created and is being orchestrated by some higher intelligence of unknown origin.

There are many variations to this concept. Some flat earth advocates contend the dome over earth itself is a holographic, three-dimensional image that portrays depth. While this theory and its variants can create intriguing discussion and debate, there is no evidence to support them and much evidence to discredit them.

A Universal Scientific Conspiracy?

I have friends who are strong believers in Jesus and believe in sound biblical doctrine, but they also believe that the earth is a flat disc and that the Bible and science both prove it. They believe NASA is deceiving the population by using photographs that are computer-generated images created to give the illusion that the universe exists.

Likewise, they hold to the belief that the Apollo program was a hoax, and that the moon landing was filmed and orchestrated inside a studio to deceive the public into thinking that man had actually landed on the moon.

It is difficult to comprehend that all the space agencies from major countries would be in a conspiracy with NASA, because many of the countries with independent space programs, satellites, and space stations are considered to be an enemy to the United States, of which NASA is a part.

What Does Science Say?

In the year 350 BC, Aristotle declared that the earth was a sphere. With limited scientific equipment at his disposal, he observed that the constellations that could be seen in the sky moved as you traveled farther away from the equator. Over the next 100 years, Aristarchus of Samos became the first man of science to declare that the earth revolved around the sun, and Eratosthenes accurately measured the circumference of the earth.

When Jesus was on the earth, it was well understood by the scientific minds of the day that the earth was a sphere that rotated around the sun.

The captains of the great sea-going vessels of centuries past did not believe the world was flat. Sailors have always known there is a curvature to the earth since it appeared their ships lowered as they sailed into the distance. The curvature was obvious.

My wife's grandfather, Charles Litterer, was a NASA scientist. He was a great patriot who served in both World Wars. When we visited him at his NASA facility, he always wore a white shirt with a narrow black tie and had a pocket protector containing a couple of scientific instruments.

He was an amazing man who was extremely intelligent. Several times while visiting him at his office at NASA, he showed us the wiring he had designed in the Apollo 8 space capsule. He was a friend of the astronauts, and even members of the moon landing crew came to his retirement party.

He was not a conspiracy theorist, he was not an atheist, he believed in God, and he understood science. And with all his knowledge, to him it was humorous that anyone would think the earth was a flat disc floating in space.

Recently, I had a discussion with a Christian friend who, as an astronaut, has circled the earth many times. When I mentioned the theory of the flat earth to him, he could not help but smile and shake his head. While some conspiracy theories may have some validity, this one can be easily put to rest. He knows the earth is not flat because he has seen it as a sphere with his own eyes.

I also believe the earth is not flat but is a spherical planet circling a star we call the sun in a solar system that is within the Milky Way Galaxy.

What Does the Bible Say about Flat Earth?

I have in my library several books and documents sent to me from individuals and ministers who advocate a flat earth. One of the major problems with the concept and theory that the earth is flat is that many flat earth advocates have only a pseudo understanding of science. While they quote Bible verses to substantiate their theory, the scriptures are taken out of context. In fact, the Bible neither proclaims the world to be flat nor a sphere.

The following scriptures are just a sampling of verses used by flat earth advocates. The scriptures are not referring to the physical shape of the planet, but to the awesome, magnificent greatness of God and His creation.

> *It is He who sits above the circle of the earth, and its inhabitants are like grasshoppers, who stretches out the heavens like a curtain, and spreads them out like a tent to dwell in.*
>
> ISAIAH 40:22

> *He stretches out the north over empty space; He hangs the earth on nothing.*
>
> JOB 26:7

When He prepared the heavens, I was there, when He drew a circle on the face of the deep.

PROVERBS 8:27

Who cover Yourself with light as with a garment, who stretch out the heavens like a curtain. He lays the beams of His upper chambers in the waters, who makes the clouds His chariot, who walks on the wings of the wind.

PSALM 104:2-3

As a Christian, do not allow the flat earth theory, or the discredit of it, to become an obsession that distracts you from the revelation of the gospel. While it may be an interesting subject to research, you must always remember that belief or non-belief in a flat earth does not determine your salvation. Your eternal life is determined by one thing only—your belief in Jesus Christ as your Lord and Savior.

If you confess with your mouth the Lord Jesus and believe in your heart that God has raised Him from the dead, you will be saved. For with the heart one believes unto righteousness, and with the mouth con-fession is made unto salvation.

ROMANS 10:9-10

Chapter 12

Ghosts

A few years ago, my wife, Loretta, and I were traveling through Arkansas and needed a place to stay for the night, so we stopped at a hotel in Eureka Springs. It was an older hotel, but it was obvious it had been upgraded, although it still had its quaint look.

Upon entering our room after checking in, I could hear a commotion in the hallway. On my investigation, I found a camera crew and someone who appeared to be a journalist with a microphone. When I inquired, they told me they were from the Syfy Channel and were doing a documentary on the most haunted hotels in America. It seems that this hotel in a past century was a treatment facility for cancer and other ailments and several people had mysteriously died there.

After leaving the hotel, I researched and discovered that the hotel also had what they called "ghost tours." This brings us to the questions: Do ghosts actually exist and what does the Bible say on this subject?

First, let's define what is meant by the word *ghosts*. The definition and terminology used today would imply that a ghost is a disembodied spirit, the slightly visible transparent image of a human who has lived and died, and for some reason is restricted to this physical earthly plane to complete a task or communicate a message to someone still living.

Biblically speaking, a ghost of this terminology does not exist. However, a scripture used by ghost theorists is Matthew 14:26. This is when Jesus told His disciples (who saw Him walking on the water) that He was not a "ghost" as they had feared. Since He did not rebuke them for saying they thought He was a ghost, many have used this scripture as proof that ghosts actually exist.

However, in the original Greek language of the New Testament, the word *ghost* and *spirit* are synonymous. The Greek word is *pneuma*. That is why you will find that some versions of the Bible say the *Holy Ghost* while other versions say the *Holy Spirit* when talking about the third member of the Trinity.

> *Now in the fourth watch of the night Jesus went to them, walking on the sea. And when the disciples saw Him walking on the sea, they were troubled, saying,* **"It is a ghost!"** *And they cried out for fear. But immediately Jesus spoke to them, saying, "Be of good cheer! It is I; do not be afraid."*
> MATTHEW 14:25-27

Angels are spirits, so it would be appropriate for the disciples to think they saw an angelic being walking on the water, which could have brought them fear. That could be why Jesus did not rebuke them.

The Bible clearly tells us that when a person physically dies, their spirit either goes to Hades or to Paradise, also known as the Bosom of Abraham (Luke 16:22-23). Nowhere in the Bible is it found that the spirit of a human, which modern terminology would define as a ghost, lingers on the earth.

Which brings another question. What is it that people see when they observe something that they perceive to be a ghost? Obviously, they are seeing something, but what is it they are seeing?

Most likely they are seeing demonic beings who are on the earth because they were cast down to the earth with Satan at his rebellion. There is also the possibility that a non-believer could see an angel of God and become fearful and perceive it as a ghost simply because of their lack of spiritual discernment.

So why would the disciples be fearful if they saw an angel of God walking on the water? Why would they be afraid? Much like the shepherds were told not to be fearful when the angelic host appeared to them at the birth of Jesus, the disciples had to be told, "Do not be afraid." Why? Probably because of the overwhelming appearance and magnificence of the angels.

But on the other hand, if they saw a demonic spirit (the spirit of a fallen angel), of course they would be afraid. Demonic spirits would be distorted and hideous and operate in the realm of fear. The bottom line is this: Ghosts, as defined in current vernacular through theater, movies, and novels, do not exist.

But angels, both of God and fallen, do exist and there are many biblical accounts of them being seen by natural eyes.

Any time a spirit brings fear by appearing as a haunted or grotesque image, it is from the enemy and not of God, but it also is not a disembodied human spirit left wandering on the earth. Beings appearing as ghosts are spirits, but not human spirits. Ghosts are NEVER human spirits. Christians are warned to NEVER participate in any activity (séance) that would attempt to conjure up a spirit from the dead. Some do this as seemingly innocent entertainment, but it can bring deadly results.

Inviting Demons to Church

Many years ago, after attending a Christian university and majoring in theology, my wife and I joined a small denominational church of about 300 members. Even though I was quite young at the time, I was asked to become the leader of the men's fellowship within the church. I was honored, so I accepted.

I thought that I had been asked because of my vast knowledge of the Bible. After all, I had been a Bible student at a Christian university. However, I later found out that they had asked most of the men in the church and they had all declined. I was their last resort. It was a humbling discovery.

Anyway, as director of the men's fellowship, I was automatically put on the church planning committee, and I anxiously awaited the first planning meeting.

The meeting was in the basement of the parsonage. The committee consisted of the Women's Missionary Union leader, the Sunday School superintendent, the chairman of the board of deacons, the pastor's wife, and me.

The pastor's wife was the committee chairman who opened the meeting by asking what progress had been made concerning the Halloween party for the youth of the church. Several suggestions were discussed, but after each suggestion the pastor's wife would make the same comment, "Last year the party was so good. How can we top it this year?" It seemed as though every recommendation made did not measure up to the previous year's party.

Since this was my first committee meeting, I wanted to keep quiet, but my curiosity got the best of me. I asked, "What did the church do last year that is so difficult to top?"

The pastor's wife leaned over and placing her hand on my arm said, "Last year we got a large round table and brought it down here to the parsonage basement. We covered it with a white tablecloth, lit candles, brought in all the teenagers in the church and had a séance. It was great!"

I couldn't believe my ears. It was my first and my last committee meeting.

How can we truly believe the Word of God and knowingly worship Satan? What an abomination!

Apparently, some Christians see nothing wrong with Halloween parties in the church or allowing children to dress and imitate witches, vampires, and demonic beings. Has the modern church become so humanistic that it sees nothing wrong with demon worship? Children should be taught to imitate and emulate *God*—not the world of the occult.

Beloved, do not imitate what is evil, but what is good. He who does good is of God, but he who does evil has not seen God.

3 John 11

Therefore be imitators of God as dear children.

Ephesians 5:1

Satanic Con Game

When people gather for a séance in order to speak to a departed person through a medium who is channeling their communication through a distorted voice, what is actually occurring? The spirit and voice are not from a departed human. It is either from the trickery of man to deceive and manipulate the living, or it is demonic. It is a type of satanic con game. The Bible teaches us that human spirits that have passed into Paradise or Hades are restricted, and unable to communicate with the living (Luke 16:26).

What is a "familiar spirit"? It is a demonic spirit that observes the living and has obtained knowledge that can be revealed or channeled through a witch or medium giving the illusion that they are the spirit of someone who has died. For this reason, the Bible says that contacting a medium to conjure up the dead is strictly forbidden, and the consequences of doing this were fatal. To speak to a familiar spirit that is pretending to be the spirit of someone departed brings confusion, deception, and destruction.

What Does the Bible Say About Ghosts?

To become obsessed with ghosts and paranormal manifestations is another distraction from the enemy. For a Christian who is seeking answers from the spirit world, their only Source is the Holy Spirit who will guide them in all truth and reveal things to come (John 16:13). A Christian should NEVER seek the kingdom of darkness for answers.

Give no regard to mediums and familiar spirits; do not seek after them, to be defiled by them: I am the LORD your God.

LEVITICUS 19:31

And the person who turns to mediums and familiar spirits, to prostitute himself with them, I will set My face against that person and cut him off from his people.

LEVITICUS 20:6

So Saul died for his unfaithfulness which he had committed against the LORD, because he did not keep the word of the LORD, and also because he consulted a medium for guidance.

1 CHRONICLES 10:13

Shapeshifters

A favorite character in modern fantasy and science fiction movies is shapeshifters. The concept of shapeshifting is based in mythology, folklore, and speculative fiction. It is the ability to physically transform its appearance into another being or object. These fictional beings have the ability to change their physical appearance so dramatically that they appear as completely different entities.

An example would be that a shapeshifter might appear as a bear, then moments later appear as a giraffe or a human. While these stories are definitely drawn from fantasy, the question we may ask is this: Is it a reality that a being can change its appearance and appear as something completely different from what it actually is?

Biblically speaking, there are beings recorded in the Bible that can change their appearance. We could call them a type of spiritual shapeshifter. While shapeshifters as portrayed in modern science fiction media are bizarre and extreme, it does reflect a spiritual truth that some spirit beings can change their appearance.

It's interesting that Satan himself has several different appearances described in Scripture. First, he was a cherub in heaven—powerful and beautiful (Ezekiel 28:14). After being expelled from heaven, he appeared as a serpent in the Garden of Eden when he spoke to Eve (Genesis 3:1). In the book of Revelation, it reveals that he was a dragon and a devil (Revelation 12:9). Second Corinthians 11:14 says that sometimes he even transforms himself into an angel of light. However, regardless of his appearance, he is still Satan and only appears to be something else.

Remember, Satan is a fallen angel, so if he has the ability to change his appearance, how much more is it possible for the angels of God (who obviously have greater power than fallen angels) to change their appearance? We know from Scripture that angels appeared in the heavens as glorious, heavenly beings when announcing the birth of Jesus to the shepherds. But as discussed earlier in this book, angels also appeared as men when they traveled to Lot's house in Sodom. But to the 185,000 Assyrians who were killed in one night by one angel, the angel must have appeared as a warrior (2 Kings 19:35).

When Jesus returns to catch away the church, Christians will go through a type of change as our resurrected bodies are transformed. At that point, in a moment, in the twinkling of an eye, we will be changed and receive our glorified bodies that are no longer restricted by the earthly rule of physics. This is a permanent change by God Himself and is *not* shapeshifting.

> *In a moment, in the twinkling of an eye, at the last trumpet. For the trumpet will sound, and the dead will be raised incorruptible, and we shall be changed. For this corruptible must put on incorruption, and this mortal must put on immortality.*
>
> 1 CORINTHIANS 15:52-53

The Bible teaches that at our transformation in the catching away of the church, we will be like Jesus is (1 John 3:2). We do not become gods, but we take our rightful place, which was God's intention from the beginning when He created us in His likeness and image. In Bible terms, we are transformed into the image of Christ (2 Corinthians 3:18).

Demonic Possession Is Not Shapeshifting

When a person receives Jesus as their Lord and Savior and becomes "born again," the Holy Spirit (the Spirit of God Himself) moves inside of them to live permanently. Because of this, a demonic spirit cannot fully possess a Christian. Of course, evil spirits can torment and oppress a Christian who allows it, but they can never fully possess a Christian. The Bible says that God is light and in Him is no darkness (1 John 1:5). Christians cannot be possessed by a demon because the Holy Spirit already possesses them.

However, non-believers living without the Holy Spirit can allow themselves to easily be fully possessed. When a demonic spirit fully possesses a person, they can literally change the physical features of that person. There have been times when a demon-possessed person was unrecognizable by their own family because their facial appearance had been so radically changed. Their strength can be increased way beyond normal.

Early in my ministry, I encountered a small, young demon-possessed girl that took six adult men to restrain, and they were extremely bruised when it was over. However, this is not shape-shifting, it is body modification and should not be confused with the shapeshifting concept. A grotesque demon-possessed person is still a person, they have not changed into another entity, their appearance was just altered.

While fantasy stories of shapeshifters in literature and theater are fictitious, the concept of changing appearance does appear in Scripture. However, even though the church will be transformed into glorified bodies, there is no evidence of humanity being able to change into another being. For humanity, shapeshifting must remain in the realm of folklore and science fiction. Mankind has never been, is not, and will never be shapeshifters.

Summary

According to the Bible, spirit beings—good and bad—do exist and can manifest themselves in the physical realm in various forms. Christians have been given a gift from God by way of the Holy Spirit called discerning of spirits (1 Corinthians 12:10). With this gift, a spirit can be identified as good or evil. And if evil, by using the authority given to the church, there should be no fear.

Chapter 13

What Is the Multiverse?

The term *multiverse* is both ambiguous and includes diverse definitions.

From a Christian perspective, the heavens are multilayered. Paul speaks of three heavens, the first being the atmosphere around the earth, and the third being the Paradise of God where the saints of God live until the return of Jesus. The ancient Book of Levi that was found in the Dead Sea Scrolls, refers to seven heavens.

Scripture tells us that Jesus ascended far above all the heavens, which further reveals that the heavens have a border and are not limitless (Ephesians 4:10). Psalm 113:4-6 also refers to an area above the heavens. Could this biblical revelation imply that the universe itself has limits to its size? Is it possible that the heavens are not measured in distance but are dimensional and there could be limits to the number of dimensions that exist?

The secular definition of multiverse is the hypothetical set of all the universes that exist. Within them they consist of the entirety of all space, time, matter, information, and all physical laws. Within the multiverse are different universes called parallel universes, flat universes, alternate universes, multiple universes, and plane universes, along with other variations.

The subject of boundaries to the heavens is explored in greater detail in Chapter 15 titled, "Heaven, Hell, and Eternity."

Two Main Theories

There are two main theories concerning the multiverse. The first implies multiple, infinite universes that exist simultaneously. While this concept of multiple universes has been discussed throughout history all the way back to Greek philosophy, it has never yet been proven, and by its very nature is considered by many scientists to be an impossibility. They say multiple infinite universes cannot exist simultaneously and also be infinite—resulting in an unsolvable paradox. True or not, it is untestable making it unprovable.

The second multiverse theory is the concept of one universe consisting of multidimensions. According to the Bible, this is not a theory, but a spiritual reality. God is multidimensional and so is our existence with Him.

This theory parallels many of the truths of the Bible as the Bible is a very multi-dimensional book. In the same way that the universe contains dark matter, which cannot be seen but can be measured by its effect on gravity and light, the Bible describes an unseen spiritual world that can be measured by its effect on what we see in the natural realm.

Multiple Dimensions

The statement made in 2 Corinthians 4:18 clearly states that everything we see is made from what we don't see. Mark 11:23 tells us that what is spoken in the physical realm travels into the spiritual realm of the unseen, and as a result, these spoken words alter the physical dimension.

> *While we do not look at the things which are seen, but at the things which are not seen. For the things which are seen are temporary, but the things which are not seen are eternal.*
>
> 2 CORINTHIANS 4:18

> *For assuredly, I say to you, whoever says to this mountain, "Be removed and be cast into the sea," and does not doubt in his heart, but believes that those things he says will be done, he will have whatever he says.*
>
> MARK 11:23

While in the wilderness, the Hebrews complained about the manna (food) provided by God each day. Interestingly, their words in the physical realm traveled into the unseen spiritual realm and were heard by God (Numbers 11:1-10).

Unseen Dimensions

There are hidden mysteries in unseen dimensions that can only be revealed by the Holy Spirit.

But as it is written: "Eye has not seen, nor ear heard, nor have entered into the heart of man the things which God has prepared for those who love Him." **But God has revealed them to us** *through His Spirit. For the Spirit searches all things, yes, the deep things of God.*

1 CORINTHIANS 2:9-10

The Bible says that many unusual miracles took place at the hands of Paul (Acts 19:11). We must never forget that as long as we are in the Church Age waiting for the return of Jesus, we can experience unusual miracles in the same way Paul the apostle did.

However, when you experience something unusual and unexplained, you must remember that everything you see comes from the realm of the unseen dimension. Any unusual unexplained experience will either be from the unseen kingdom of light or the unseen kingdom of darkness. Both kingdoms are multidimensional and discerning of spirits (by the Holy Spirit) is required to know the difference.

With the gift of discerning of spirits, the Holy Spirit will reveal the nature of a spirit whether it is of God or not (1 Corinthians 12:10). A miracle from God, whether it is normal or unusual, will always have a purpose and will always glorify Him. A false miracle will exalt the miracle worker and tend to lead people away from the purpose of God.

Crossing Dimensions

My office overlooks the Lake of the Ozarks that has 1,300 miles of shoreline. It is a freshwater lake that is a major tourist attraction. This resort area is also the home to one of Missouri's largest state parks that is a natural habitat for thousands of wild deer. In the area surrounding the lake, it is a common occurrence for deer to run onto the highway and be struck by oncoming vehicles. When driving around the lake area, everyone is watchful for deer.

With this in mind, a very unusual event occurred recently as Loretta and I were traveling at full speed on a divided highway. A large deer with a full head of antlers suddenly ran toward my vehicle and it looked like there would be an imminent impact on the passenger side of the car. My wife gasped as she braced for the collision.

But instead of hitting the car, the deer passed through our car in front of me and exited on the driver's side. It was so close that I could see its fur on the dashboard in front of my steering wheel. I felt as though I could reach out and touch it. The deer literally ran through my vehicle.

Fortunately, I had a witness in the car and we watched as the image passed through the car. We both saw it happen. I honestly believe that as Loretta and I prayed protection over our travels that morning that the angels of God protected us and our vehicle from harm.

I have no logical explanation for this event. However, I do have some thoughts. I believe it was a momentary dimensional shift as the deer went through my vehicle. In other words, the deer was a living animal, but miraculously dematerialized as it approached our car and then re-materialized on the other side, protecting my vehicle, and possibly saving our lives.

A Very Unusual Miracle

I have a close friend who has spent his life ministering the gospel around the world and has also served as a professor and dean at multiple Christian universities. I know him to be a man of integrity and truth and not prone to "weird things." However, he privately shared an event with me that took place at one of his crusades.

While he was teaching from the platform, two young girls were creating a disturbance in the congregation. Their plan was to ridicule and disrupt. One of them had an empty soft drink bottle in her hand and was loudly proclaiming that God was not real. However, she went on to say if He were real, she could put Him in a bottle and contain Him.

With that statement she stuck her finger into the neck of the bottle and her finger immediately began to swell. In a mocking way, she approached the platform and asked for help.

The minister (my friend) reached out and took her hand into his hand. With her finger stuck tightly inside the bottle, he prayed for the young girl's deliverance. He watched as her finger dematerialized from within the bottle and re-materialized outside the bottle. Needless to say, the girl and her friend became believers that day.

How did this happen? Is there any biblical record of something like this occurring? Yes, there is. This is simply an unusual miracle, like by the hands of Paul.

Altered Physics

Another very unusual miracle took place after the resurrection of Jesus when the disciples were gathered in a locked room. Jesus was outside the locked door and moments later stood among the disciples inside the locked room (John 20:19). The Bible doesn't explain how it happened, only that it did happen. And it is recorded that it happened at least twice (John 20:26). Did Jesus dematerialize, or did the wall become porous enough for Him to walk through it? Either way, physics were altered, and Jesus passed through the wall.

> *On the evening of that day, the first day of the week, the doors being locked where the disciples were for fear of the Jews, Jesus came and stood among them and said to them, "Peace be with you."*
>
> JOHN 20:19 ESV

We must never forget that the God who created physics can alter physics.

Summary

The Bible makes no reference to multiple universes, but is clear that multiple dimensions exist, and it is from the unseen dimension of heaven that miracles are seen on earth.

Chapter 14

CLIMATE CHANGE

*The Scriptures also say, "In the beginning, Lord, you were the one who laid the foundation of the earth and created the heavens. They will all disappear and **wear out like clothes**, but you will last forever. You will **roll them up like a robe and change them like a garment**. But you are always the same, and you will live forever."*

HEBREWS 1:10-12 CEV

*While the earth remains, seedtime and harvest, cold and heat, summer and winter, day and night, **shall not cease**.*

GENESIS 8:22 ESV

A great controversy that has arisen in modern times is the fear by some that the lifestyle of humans living on the earth will change the climate and cause the earth to eventually become uninhabitable. There is an entire generation that has been taught to believe that the destruction of the earth by mankind is progressing at such a rapid rate that this generation will be the last generation that will experience trees and green grass. They sincerely believe this!

This fear has been so radically preached that even things not connected to energy production or atmospheric pollution are being targeted as a cause of climate change. This has been carried to such an extreme that even bovine flatulence made national news claiming it causes as much as 15 percent of global greenhouse gas emissions each year. It has also been reported that coffee, due to the growing of the coffee beans, as well as the transporting, roasting, grinding, and brewing, is a major contributor to climate change every year!

This mindset appears to be driven by fear and is used politically to manipulate the public. Fear is a spiritual force that, by its very nature, will bring destruction and the inability to think rationally.

When I was young, I was taught that climate change was inevitable. The difference is back then our professors were teaching that the earth was getting ready to go through another ice age. There was great concern because everything scientific seemed to be pointing that way. It's so interesting to see that professors in the same universities are still teaching that there will be climate change; however, they are now teaching that the earth is warming, and could become a desert.

Throughout the planet's history, earth's climate has changed dramatically, with the climate of ancient earth being either much warmer, or much colder than it is today. The study of ancient climate is called paleoclimatology, which predates the invention of modern meteorological instruments.

The change of climate evolved in ancient Egypt and Mesopotamia because these areas experienced prolonged periods of droughts or floods. In the 17th century, Robert Hooke theorized that the fossils of giant turtles found in southwest England were a result of the climate once being much warmer. He thought this could be a result of the earth shifting on its axis. Others believed these fossils occurred because of Noah's flood that is recorded in the Bible.

Heinrich Schwabe, an astronomer in the early 19th century, became very concerned about how the sun affected the earth's climate. With discoveries of natural changes in the earth's past relating to the greenhouse effect, the scientific field of paleo-climatology began to have greater influence.

Just a few short decades ago, a radical movement took place as protestors threw paint on SUV automobiles because they heard someone state that SUVs use more fuel than a regular automobile.

During this same time, there were animal activists who tossed paint onto fur coats, with the idea they were protecting animals from having their skin used as clothing. Many of the "fur coats" were not fur, but synthetics, while the activists throwing the paint had leather wallets and leather shoes made from animal skins.

The weirdness of humanity seems to go through cycles. In a short time, these protests fade away and then looking back, they are ridiculous.

Presidential candidate Al Gore stated on December 14, 2009, that there was a 75 percent chance that the entire Arctic polar ice cap could be completely ice-free within the next five to seven years. At the time, it sounded very reasonable to some, but it never happened. Looking back, it's humorous. Likewise, that will be the fate of climate change.

What Does the Bible Say about Climate Change?

Here is what the Bible says about the condition of the earth in the future: When Jesus returns, people will be eating and drinking and giving in marriage (Matthew 24:37-39). The implication is that daily life will be going on as normal on the earth. Genesis 8:22 confirms that the earth will have continuous winters and summers without ceasing. Seedtime and harvest will continue, and there will be a balance between cold and heat while the earth remains. This tells us there should be no panic over the earth being destroyed by mankind before the return of Jesus.

On another note, after Jesus does return to set up His kingdom, we know that the earth will continue on for another thousand years (during the millennial reign of Jesus) with seedtime and harvest, cold and heat, summer and winter, and day and night. After the millennial reign has ended, there will be a judgment (great white throne judgment), and God will eradicate all evil from the earth forever.

In Revelation 21:1, John had a vision of a new heaven and earth. The Greek word for *new* is *kainos*, which does not mean a different heaven and earth but refurbished. The *heaven* in this scripture is referring to is the first heaven, which is the atmosphere of the earth. Peter said that the earth would be reserved for fire.

*But the heavens and the earth which are now preserved by the same word, **are reserved for fire** until the day of judgment and perdition of ungodly men.*

2 PETER 3:7

What does this mean? It means there will be a cleansing of the earth by God Himself, with a refurbished, renewed earth and atmosphere. This will happen in God's timing after the great white throne judgment at the end of the millennium. Because death will no longer be a factor for those living in flesh-and-blood bodies (Revelation 21:4), and because God will tabernacle (live) with mankind (Revelation 21:3), the new earth will be inhabited by mankind for eternity.

*But the day of the Lord will come as a thief in the night, in which the heavens will pass away with a great noise, and the elements will melt with fervent heat; **both the earth and the works that are in it will be burned up.***

*Therefore, since all these things will be dissolved, what manner of persons ought you to be in holy conduct and godliness, looking for and hastening the coming of the day of God, **because of which the heavens will be dissolved, being on fire, and the elements will melt with fervent heat?** Nevertheless we, according to His promise, **look for new heavens and a new earth** in which righteousness dwells.*

2 PETER 3:10-13

Should we be concerned about the condition of the earth? Of course! We should restrict the use of pollutants in the air, water, and ground that are dangerous. Yes, we have a responsibility to tend and keep the earth (Genesis 2:15). Although we know the earth is aging (Hebrews 1:10-12), we should not allow fear to cause us to make foolish and bizarre decisions that affect our lifestyle and restrict us from living the abundant life promised to us in the Word of God (John 10:10).

Once again, according to the Bible, there will be continuous winter and summer, cold and heat, until God refurbishes the earth at least 1,007 years from now (after the millennium). So why do people choose to worry about something God has completely under His control? In the words of Jesus, "Do not worry about tomorrow" (Matthew 6:34).

Remember...

While the earth remains, seedtime and harvest, cold and heat, winter and summer, and day and night **shall not cease.**

Genesis 8:22

Chapter 15

HEAVEN, HELL, AND ETERNITY

The religions and cults of the world all refer to a distant place of eternal peace. The Hindus call it "Svarga," the Buddhists call it "Sagga," and the Muslims call it "Jannah." The ancient Canaanites called it the land of Mot, while the Christians and Jews simply call it heaven.

HEAVEN

However, unlike the abode of the dead in cults and false religions, the Christian heaven is a real place. According to the Christian Bible, we are given details of its location, its design, its purpose, and how it can be accessed.

First of all, there is a literal place called heaven. Heaven is a beautiful place, and its beauty cannot be described in an earthly language. There was a time when the heavens did not exist, because Genesis 1:1 tells us the time of their creation. In the beginning, God created multiple heavens. Of course, in the beginning was not the beginning of God. He has always existed in eternity past which has no beginning. The heavens and the earth were created for God's eternal plan for mankind.

Multi-Dimensional Heaven

It's interesting to note in this passage in Genesis 1:1, the Hebrew word for heaven is plural, which lets us know that there are multiple areas and dimensions within the realm of heaven. The apostle Paul indicated that he visited the third heaven, while the Testament of Levi (found in the Dead Sea Scrolls) indicates there are seven heavens.

Within the heavens there is the holy city, an area referred to as the heavenly Jerusalem. There are, of course, other areas of heaven, one of which is Paradise, which is the holding place for the departed righteous residing in their spirit bodies. These departed saints are waiting for the rapture when they will receive their resurrected, glorified bodies. The size of Paradise (which is also known as the Bosom of Abraham) is not defined in Scripture. Likewise, the area outside the heavenly Jerusalem is not given a specific size.

The Heavenly City

The Hebrew word for Jerusalem is *Yerushalayim.* Hebrew words ending in "ayim" designate two of something. Within the name of Jerusalem, it is stated that there are two Jerusalems.

In the government buildings in Israel, there are paintings and murals that depict Jerusalem with an image of the heavenly city in the clouds above. It is well understood scripturally that there are two Jerusalems—the earthly Jerusalem and the heavenly Jerusalem. Although these two cities are separate, they are one. One is on the earth, and one is above it in the heavens. They are *Yerushalayim*.

Jerusalem is built as a city that is compact together.
PSALM 122:3

The Bible talks of the heavenly Jerusalem and the New Jerusalem. Both are the dwelling place of God the Father, and both are the dwelling place of the saints, but they do not exist simultaneously. The heavenly Jerusalem has been in existence from the creation of the heavens and is the heavenly capital city that is in existence now. The heavenly Jerusalem will continue until the end of the millennium, until after the great white throne judgment, and until death has been totally defeated for all eternity.

Then the heavenly Jerusalem will be refurbished and will descend out of heaven upon the earthly Jerusalem and will thereafter be called the New Jerusalem. This is the place that is the home of God, and it is the place that Jesus is preparing for those who believe. The New Jerusalem will be the eternal home of the saints (Revelation 21:9-10,27). While the saints of God will have their home base in this new city, travel beyond comprehension and discoveries beyond our current understanding will be available.

Now I saw a new heaven and a new earth, for the first heaven and the first earth had passed away. Also

there was no more sea. Then I, John, saw the holy city,
*New Jerusalem, **coming down out of heaven from***
***God**, prepared as a bride adorned for her husband.*
REVELATION 21:1-2

The Bible tells us the specific size of the New Jerusalem which comes down out of heaven after the 1,000-year millennial reign of Jesus on the earth. The Bible says that the length, width, and height will be 12,000 *furlongs*. In the original manuscripts, the word translated as furlong was actually the Greek word *stadia*. And 12,000 stadia is about 1,380 miles. Many scholars round this off to 1,500 miles.

Not only are the four walls of the New Jerusalem 1,500 miles long, they are also 1,500 miles high. How high is this? The International Space Station in outer space is only 250 miles above the earth. The New Jerusalem will extend six times farther into space than the space station. The size of the city is so massive that if it were hovering over North America, it would cover almost half of the continental United States.

The future occupants of the New Jerusalem will be in resurrected, glorified bodies and gravity will not affect them. So the exact makeup of all the structure and our existence in the New Jerusalem could possibly be beyond our finite imagination. But we do know that it will be a glorious place without a temple because the Son will illuminate the city (Revelation 21:22-23). Jesus said that He and the Father are one (John 10:30) and God is light (1 John 1:5).

The secular world says that Jerusalem (*Yerushalayim*) is the home to three world religions—Judaism, Christianity, and Islam. That is not true. It's interesting to note that Jerusalem is not mentioned even once in the Islamic holy book, the Koran.

Jerusalem is the holy city to only one true God. His name is *Yod Hey Vav Hey*, and He sent His Son to redeem mankind. There is only one true God—and Jerusalem is His holy city.

> *For the* LORD *has chosen Jerusalem; he has desired it for his home. "This is my resting place forever,"*
> *he said. "I will live here, for this is the home I desired."*
> PSALM 132:13-14 NLT

Heavenly Portals

The angels that stayed loyal to God have full access between heaven and earth. In the Old Testament, Jacob saw angels ascending and descending from heaven (Genesis 28:12). In his way of thinking they were using a ladder. In more current terminology, we would call this a portal.

Jesus told Nathanael that he would see angels ascending and descending from heaven (John 1:51), and there are many visitations of angels recorded by the apostles in the New Testament (such as Acts 5:18-20; Acts 8:26; Acts 10:30-32). Because of this, we know that in our current dispensation of time, angels from heaven can access the earth and be messengers for God and return to heaven. They don't need a passport or a visa because they have full access.

*And He said to him, "Most assuredly, I say to you, hereafter you shall see heaven open, and **the angels of God ascending and descending** upon the Son of Man."*
JOHN 1:51

The Expanse of the Heavens

We must remember that after the millennium the heavenly Jerusalem will be upgraded to the New Jerusalem. But the New Jerusalem is not the entirety of heaven—but is a city within heaven. The Bible doesn't specifically say so, but the implication is that within heaven there could be multiple cities with the New Jerusalem being the capital.

To limit heaven to the confines of one relatively small area compared to the expanse of the universe, would seem to greatly restrict the future of mankind. The number of known galaxies is in the trillions with more being discovered at a rapid rate. To think that God would restrict His creation with resurrected, glorified bodies to one city limits His greatness.

When God said, "Let there be light" in Genesis 1, He never commanded light to stop. Physical light that contains photons is merely a physical manifestation of true light. Light never ceases. The image received by a telescope from a star that is millions of light years away is actually the light given off by the star millions of light years ago. The light never ceases; it continues eternally. The manifestation of God as light reveals His eternal existence that never diminishes or ends. Man has been unable to visually see the limits of the universe, which reveals this truth: God and His creation are beyond human comprehension.

Above the Heavens

Does heaven fill the entire universe? Scripturally, that's an unanswered question, but we do know that heaven itself does have boundaries. How do we know this? Because Ephesians 4:10 says that Jesus, after His resurrection, ascended far *above* all the heavens. Here again is a reference to there being multiple heavens; but regardless of how many there are, whether there are three, seven, or more, they have a boundary and Jesus ascended, not just above, but *far above* all the heavens.

> *He who descended is also the One who ascended far above all the heavens, that He might fill all things.*
>   EPHESIANS 4:10

So this raises yet another question. What is beyond the heavens? Again we go to the Bible for the answer. We are told that beyond the heavens is the glory of God. What is the glory of God? His glory is the manifestation of His being and His essence. In other words, we could say that the heavens (the universe) is encapsulated by the presence of God.

> *The LORD is high above all nations, His glory above the heavens.*
>   PSALM 113:4

Your Place in Eternity

As a born-again Christian living in the New Jerusalem, you will be living in a resurrected, glorified body that is equal to the body of our Lord and Savior, Jesus Christ. Your home in the New Jerusalem cannot be compared in any way to any mansion on earth. The splendor and magnificence of what Jesus has prepared for you cannot be expressed in earthly words.

You will be an individual with individual desires and future dreams. You will have individuality because you will be given a name that only He knows (Revelation 2:17). You will have His name on your forehead (Revelation 22:4). He is yours and you are His. You will have creativity, and you will have friendships that were developed on earth and new friendships developed in heaven.

The universe and beyond will forever be yours to explore. The vastness of God is beyond description. Is it possible that there is a place in the universe where nothing has been created yet, and is just waiting for you to explore and get creative with three billion years from now? Could the universe have unexplored places or unexplored technology waiting for believers to explore and create? After all, we were created in the likeness and image of God and told to be like Him (Ephesians 5:1). He is the master Creator.

In heaven, there will never be a time of boredom or sadness. Every tear will be wiped away. Death and the fear of loss will be eliminated. Eternity and God's kingdom are endless. Our life is eternal so there will never be an end to our experience of the joy He has prepared for us. Your creativity, your travel, and your abilities will be so far beyond that of natural man that boredom on any level will be an absolute impossibility!

Getting to Heaven

According to the Bible, in this current dispensation called the Church Age (age of grace or the last days), there is only one way for a human to gain eternal access into the place called heaven, and that is to believe and receive Jesus Christ as Lord and Savior.

Satan is a liar and a deceiver (John 8:44; 2 Corinthians 11:13-15). He often counterfeits the things of God in order to lead people astray. Why do all the religions and cults of the world have a place like heaven, but give it a different name with a different way of gaining entrance? It's simply because the enemy wants to derail and divert man to another way that has only the illusion of eternal peace, but which is actually the pathway to hell.

HELL

The Old Testament was written in Hebrew. The Hebrew word s*heol* in many versions of the English Bible is translated as "grave" and is understood to be the temporary abode of the dead in the underworld.

The New Testament was written in Koine Greek. There are three Greek words in the original *Texus Receptus* manuscript that are translated into English as *hell*. These three words are *hades, gehenna, and tartarus.* Each of these three words have a different origin and a different meaning, but all have the same ending result. They are a place of torment and punishment after death.

Hades

And I also say to you that you are Peter, and on this rock I will build My church, and the gates of Hades shall not prevail against it.

MATTHEW 16:18

"When Jesus and His disciples were near the town of Caesarea Phillipi, he asked them, 'What do people say about the Son of Man?'" (Matthew 16:13 CEV). When Simon Peter answered and said, "You are the Christ [Messiah], the Son of the Living God," Jesus blessed him. Then Jesus told him, "You are Peter, and on this rock I will build My church, and the gates of Hades shall not prevail against it" (Matthew 16:18).

It's interesting that Jesus chose the word *hades*. Hades was the name of the Greek god of the underworld, which was the abode of the dead in Greek mythology. This mythological place of the dead was named Hades (Pluto) and ruled by Hades himself along with his wife, Persephone.

At the time of Jesus, the Greek word *hades* generally replaced the Hebrew word *sheol*, which simply meant *the abode of the dead*. However, in New Testament scripture, Hades represented not only death, but a place of torment with fire.

Gehenna

The Valley of Gehenna surrounded ancient Jerusalem from the west and southwest. It meets and merges with the Kidron Valley. It's first mentioned as part of the border between the tribes of Judah and Benjamin (Joshua 15:8). In Jewish rabbinic literature, *gehinnom* became associated with divine punishment and was the destination of the wicked to pay for their sins. It was different from the term *sheol*, which was a more neutral term for the abode of the dead. The King James Version translates both *sheol* and *gehenna* as hell because they are both the abode of the dead.

There are many writings and accounts of Gehenna being described as outside the city walls. It was a place where Baal was worshiped and children were sacrificed to the pagan god Molech. There was also a time when it was a place where waste and trash were dumped and fire burned continuously.

Of the twelve occurrences of the use of the word *gehenna* in the New Testament, it is definitely referring to a place of torment after physical death.

Tartarus

The Greek word *tartarus* is only used once in the New Testament and is translated as "hell" in the English Bible.

The word *tartarus* comes from Greek mythology. In Greek mythology, Tartarus is the deep abyss that is used as a dungeon of torment and suffering for the wicked. Tartarus is the place where, according to Plato's *Gorgias* (400 BC), souls are judged after death and divine judgment is inflicted upon the wicked.

The apostle Peter must have used this word in his writing to demonstrate the extreme nature of the punishment of those imprisoned there.

> *For if God did not spare the angels who sinned, but cast them down to hell* [Tartarus] *and delivered them into chains of darkness, to be **reserved for judgment**.*
> 2 PETER 2:4

The 200 Watchers who were the sons of God assigned to watch over mankind, deserted their assignment and mated with earthly women, which produced the Nephilim. This sin was so great in the eyes of God that they were bound and separated in the deepest part of the underworld (Tartarus). Their capture and containment are complete, and they are waiting for their judgment reserved for them at the end of the millennium. These are probably the angels that will be judged by the church (1 Corinthians 6:3).

Remember, the angels that rebelled with Lucifer have already been judged and their eternal punishment awaits them. They know their time is coming. That is why they asked Jesus, "Have You come here to torment us before the time?" when He cast Legion out of the mad man of the Gadarenes (Matthew 8:29).

Three Hells or One?

Regardless of whether the original Greek word is hades, gehenna, or tartarus, they all refer to a place of eternal punishment and torment. When Jesus was talking about the place created for the devil and his angels (Matthew 25:41), He described it as a place of everlasting fire. Jesus clearly referred to the fires of hell (gehenna) as He was teaching (Matthew 18:9).

The Reality of Hell

There are many well-known ministers who are currently teaching that a literal hell does not exist but is metaphorical. They explain this by saying that God is a good God and would never send anyone to a place called hell that is described so vividly in the Bible as a place of eternal torment and punishment. Actually, the reason hell exists is because of the love that God has for us.

How does hell fit into the concept that God is love? The answer is quite simple and actually quite logical. In the same way that Noah's flood was an act of love because it saved mankind from extinction, God will once again destroy evil as an act of love.

In the same way that prisons are built to keep murderers, thieves, and rapists separated from the general population of good people, likewise hell was created to contain Satan and his angels who rebelled.

Hell does exist and the Bible describes it as a place of punishment and eternal separation from God. It is never suggested to be metaphorical, fictional, or conceptual—it is always portrayed to be a real place with real torment.

Then he cried and said, "Father Abraham, have mercy on me, and send Lazarus that he may dip the tip of his finger in water and cool my tongue; for I am tormented in this flame." But Abraham said, "Son, remember that in your lifetime you received your good things, and likewise Lazarus evil things; but now he is comforted and you are tormented."

Luke 16:24-25

And will cast them into the furnace of fire. There will be wailing and gnashing of teeth.

Matthew 13:42

Very clearly Jesus says that the unrighteous will go away to a place of eternal punishment while the righteous go to a place of eternal life (Matthew 25:46).

Originally, hell was created for Satan and his angels (Matthew 25:41; Revelation 20:10) but was revealed in the New Testament to also be a place of punishment for those who reject Jesus Christ as their Lord and Savior.

The torment in hell is described in several passages several different ways. It is called a furnace of fire where there will be weeping and gnashing of teeth (Matthew 13:50), a place where the worm never dies, and the fire is never quenched (Mark 9:45-46). The torment that lasts forever and ever gives those who are in hell no rest, day or night (Revelation 14:11).

Hell is definitely a place to be avoided at all costs; and scripturally, the judgment of whether or not one goes to hell is determined during their life before death. There is clearly one life to live, one choice to make, and after that the judgment— good or bad, heaven or hell (Hebrews 9:27).

And as it is appointed for men to die once, but after this the judgment.

HEBREWS 9:27

So it will be at the end of the age. The angels will come forth, separate the wicked from among the just, and cast them into the furnace of fire. There will be wailing and gnashing of teeth.

MATTHEW 13:49-50

Then He will also say to those on the left hand, "Depart from Me, you cursed, into the everlasting fire prepared for the devil and his angels."

MATTHEW 25:41

And if your foot causes you to sin, cut it off. It is better for you to enter life lame, rather than having two feet, to be cast into hell, into the fire that shall never be quenched—where "Their worm does not die and the fire is not quenched."

MARK 9:45-46

And the smoke of their torment ascends forever and ever; and they have no rest day or night, who worship the beast and his image, and whoever receives the mark of his name.

REVELATION 14:11

And anyone not found written in the Book of Life was cast into the lake of fire.

REVELATION 20:15

Hell—A Place to be Avoided

God did not send His Son to condemn the world, but through Him the whole world could be saved (John 3:17). The world was already condemned, and Jesus came to make a way of escape from the impending doom of all humanity.

God loves you so much that He wants to separate evil from you. He wants to separate you from the entity (Satan) that is the source of all lying, cheating, stealing, murder, and ultimately death (John 10:10). Satan will never quit being evil. God loves you so much that He created a prison for the devil and his angels. He wants you to live in a place where evil does not exist. God's love is so powerful and so magnificent that those who believe in Him and His Son will forever be separated from those who reject and rebel against Him.

The sad thing is a lot of people reject the Lord and side with the enemy, and that means they get the same treatment as the enemy. The angels that followed Lucifer have and will receive the same punishment as Lucifer (Satan). Unfortunately, people who follow Satan will join him and his angels in their imprisoned place called hell.

God's will is that no one should perish (2 Peter 3:9) but that everyone should repent and come to know the Truth and have everlasting life. However, only those who receive the Truth will escape hell.

Some may say that this doesn't seem fair. Why would anyone be sent to a place of eternal punishment for simply rejecting God in this life? This may sound harsh to some, but the reality is this: It doesn't matter what you think. In the kingdom of God, there is a King and what the King declares is the reality that we live by. God is just, and He has proclaimed in His Word the way it is, and that's the way it is.

We must accept His prophetic proclamation and understand the seriousness of it. For this reason, we must do everything possible to evangelize and proclaim His love to a lost and dying world. If you truly love your friends and family as most people say they do, then you will do everything possible for them to escape the reality of hell and instead inherit eternal life in the glorious kingdom of God.

ETERNITY

He has made everything beautiful in its time. Also He has put eternity in their hearts, except that no one can find out the work that God does from beginning to end.

ECCLESIASTES 3:11

The concept of *eternity* by definition is infinite or unending time. In the biblical definition, eternity is a realm without beginning and without end.

God lives in eternity; and coming from an endless past, He placed a marker at creation that mankind sees as the beginning of time. Therefore, humankind has a beginning, but our existence is eternal. As a spirit with a body, your eternal existence is not in question. The only question is: Where will you be in eternity?

Scripturally, after the Second Coming of Jesus and for the next 1,000 years, mankind will be in one of three places. Some will be in heaven with glorified bodies, some will be in Hades with spirit bodies waiting for the judgment at the end of the millennial reign of Christ, and some will be in human flesh-and-blood bodies, populating the earth.

At the end of the thousand-year millennial reign, the church will continue with glorified bodies. The unrighteous dead will be resurrected for judgment, then cast into outer darkness (hell). At the end of the millennial reign of Christ, those living on the earth will have either honored the Lord or rebelled against Him as part of the army of Satan. The ones who rebelled are likewise cast into outer darkness (hell).

The Bible does not say what happens after the millennium to those who remain in human bodies and honored the Lord during the millennium, but there is a strong implication that they continue in human bodies to populate the new refurbished earth and its cleansed atmosphere.

However, one thing we know for sure. According to Revelation 21:4 at the final judgment, just before the presentation of the new heaven and earth, death will be eliminated. That simply means that from that point on throughout eternity, those living in heaven and on earth who have honored the Lord will never again experience death. This is when the promise that Jesus gave in John 3:16 is fulfilled—we experience the fullness of our eternal life.

> *...then shall be brought to pass the saying that is written: "Death is swallowed up in victory. O Death, where is your sting? O Hades, where is your victory?"*
> 1 Corinthians 15:54–55

Here's a very important truth. Your eternal existence is determined and established while you are living on the earth in your flesh-and-blood body before death or the catching away of the church. There are many biblical concepts that can be pondered and debated, but there is only one thing that determines your eternal destination and that is your relationship with Jesus Christ as your Lord and Savior.

Remember, God gives all sentient beings the gift of free choice. Lucifer and his followers had the freedom to live in Paradise or to rebel. They chose poorly and were cast out for eternity. The Watchers were sent to oversee mankind and have their abode in the heavens, but they chose poorly and were imprisoned. Adam was given the ability to live forever in the Garden God made for him, but he chose poorly and was cast out.

You have been given the ability to choose life or death. Choose wisely. Your eternity depends on it.

> *I call heaven and earth as witnesses today against you,*
> *that I have set before you life and death, blessing and*
> *cursing; therefore choose life....*
> DEUTERONOMY 30:19

Chapter 16

The Mystery of the Hebrew Language

The Bible is a prophetic book. From the beginning to the end, the Holy Scriptures reveal God's plan for the ages. The entire Bible is prophetic in nature. Ultimately every word contains revelation.

We must understand the Bible is the inspired Word of God; God wrote the Bible. The Hebrew Bible is full of mysteries, but they are not a mystery to God, and they don't have to be a mystery to us. Mysteries that are placed in God's Word are to be revealed to His people, the Christians.

The Hebrew language is unique and not like any other language. It is the language used by God Himself when He penned the Ten Commandments in stone for Moses (Exodus 31:18). It's the language specifically mentioned when Jesus spoke to Saul (the apostle Paul) from the blinding light on the road to Damascus (Acts 26:14).

The ancient sages and rabbis spoke of 70 layers or 70 dimensions to each of the 22 letters in the Hebrew alphabet. This ancient language given by God is mathematical, musical, and artistic. Not only does each letter have a color, frequency, and numeric value, but each letter also has a symbol. For example, the symbol for *Dalet,* the fourth letter of the Hebrew language, is *door.*

When used in the Holy Scriptures, Hebrew is encoded with messages that prove it is not only divinely inspired, but uniquely written with the precision that could only come from the infinite mind of God.

The Hebrew language was inserted into this earth 3,500 years ago with 2.5 million words. The Hebrew word for *computer* that we use today existed 3,500 years ago. Back then they didn't know what it meant, but the word was there. All they knew is the word meant "something that thinks for you." The spiritual principle of speaking the word before you see the manifestation is inherit in the Hebrew language (Mark 11:23).

Analog or Digital

All the languages of the world could be compared to analog recordings, but Hebrew would be like a digital recording. Let me explain.

Digital media is written in binary code. If you make a copy of a digital file, the copy will be identical to the original. On the other hand, each succeeding copy of an analog file loses quality. The Hebrew language is unchanging and eternal.

An example of an analog language is English. The meanings and spellings of the words tend to change over time. In this modern day, it would be difficult for most people to read an original copy of the King James version of the Bible as it was translated in 1611. First of all, in 1611 there were only 24 letters in the English alphabet where today we have 26. Also, simple words were spelled differently. The word *son* today was spelled *sonne* in 1611.

A Digital Copy

When a Hebrew Torah scroll is copied by a scribe, there can be no errors. Mathematical formulas are used so one small mistake makes the whole section damaged and the scribe must start over.

It is also interesting that when copying the Torah and coming to the word *Yod Hey Vav Hey*, which is translated Lord, the scribe must take a ceremonial bath (called a *mikvah*) each time before writing the name of God.

Years ago, a copper scroll of Isaiah was found that was estimated to be 1,200 years older than any previously known copy. There was discussion among scholars about how the book of Isaiah might have changed over 1,200 years. To their amazement they discovered there was no change. Great precision has been used to keep God's Word unaltered.

We should give great credit to the Jews for their dedication to keeping the Holy Scriptures accurate and unchanging. This was a direct command from God to them, and they have followed His command to the letter.

The Ezekiel Stones

On one of our trips to Israel, Loretta and I were privileged to view the Ezekiel Stones. This is a set of flat square stones that were discovered in Ezekiel's tomb 80 miles south of Baghdad. On them is written the entire book of Ezekiel. The way they were discovered and how they came to be in Israel is a miraculous story, but even more miraculous are the stones themselves. To describe all of their uniqueness would take many pages, but I want to mention the two most amazing details I found about them.

First, they are written from the viewpoint of current time. In other words, in our modern Bible when the book of Ezekiel says, "There was a king," the stones say, "There is a king." This indicates that the king was living when the stones were written. Other than the time being referred to as present time rather than past time, the entirety of the book is an exact original (digital) of the copy we have today.

The second feature that is still unexplained by archeologists and the scientific community is that the letters written in stone are in relief instead of being carved into the stone. This means the letters are raised and pulled away from the stone. The technology to do that did not exist at the time of Ezekiel, and to this day it remains a mystery as to how this was done. Archeologists and scholars are still scratching their heads in wonder.

Music from God

Sing to Him a new song; play skillfully with a shout of joy.

Psalm 33:3

The Hebrew language is not just a method of verbal and written communication, it is multidimensional. One dimension is music, and notes are actually encoded within each letter.

A Hebrew professor at a state university started a project to research the frequencies or notes associated with each Hebrew letter. There are 22 letters in the Hebrew alphabet, which covers three octaves. There were also 22 strings on King David's harp, so each string represented a Hebrew letter.

The professor fed the Hebrew letters of Psalm 23 into a computer in the order they appear in the psalm, then the computer converted the letters to frequencies. The result was that the notes of Psalm 23 created beautiful music that soothes the soul.

King David was not only the king, but he was also a skilled musician. Before he was king, he played his harp for King Saul when he was tormented by demons. As David played, the demons left the king, and his sound mind returned (1 Samuel 16:14-23). Why did the demons leave?

When David played the notes, each vibration or frequency in the air represented a Hebrew letter. Could it be that he was not just playing a melody, but he was literally playing words that contained the power to repel evil spirits? This is the power that true music from God contains.

The Hebrew language is truly miraculous. We know that God is interested in the Psalms (Luke 24:44) and they are important to Him. Praise and worship are important to God. All of creation yearns to worship Him.

God's Personal Song

Embedded in the book of Psalms in the Holy Bible is one psalm that is very unique—Psalm 119. This psalm is the longest chapter in the Bible and is near the center of the Bible (Psalm 118), but its unique quality goes far beyond that.

Psalm 119 is a song written by God that is divided into 22 stanzas with each stanza containing eight verses. Each stanza corresponds to a letter in the Hebrew alphabet, with the letters placed in alphabetical order. Beginning with the first letter *Aleph* and ending with the last letter *Tav*, this psalm takes the singer through the entire Hebrew alphabet, one letter at a time, with eight lines beginning with the same letter within that stanza. This chapter contains 176 verses.

As Christians, we believe that the entire Bible is inspired by the Holy Spirit, with each verse, chapter, and book woven together supernaturally. With this in mind, we must understand that God has a special place in His heart for the Hebrew language above all others.

It also reveals that God inspires musicians to speak His Word through melody, harmony, meter, and poetry. There are psalmists today who are led by the Holy Spirit in the same way

God led the psalmist of Psalm 119. They bring inspired songs to earth that contain messages from heaven.

Queen Esther's Prophecy Fulfilled

There are literally thousands of hidden codes within the Hebrew text of our Bible. It's interesting that some prophecies in the Bible are not seen as prophecies until their manifestation takes place, because the hidden codes cannot be discovered until after the prophetic event occurs. This confirms the supernatural accuracy of the text.

> *For nothing is secret that will not be revealed, nor anything hidden that will not be known and come to light.*
> Luke 8:17

An example of hidden codes is found in the book of Esther. First, I would like to give you a brief overview of the conditions surrounding this prophecy. In the 5th century BC, King Ahasuerus, who was the king of Persia (modern-day Iran) and reigned over 127 provinces, gave a banquet for all his officials and servants. For 180 days, he displayed the great wealth of his kingdom for all to see. After that, the king made a seven-day feast for all the people in his city.

During that feast, while intoxicated, he ordered Queen Vashti to come before him, wearing her royal crown, to reveal her beauty to his guests. According to Jewish *midrash*, it is commonly supposed that the king commanded his wife to appear nude in front of the drunken men. She refused and this made him furious. His wise men were also infuriated and suggested to the king that he depose the queen.

Because of the king's displeasure with Queen Vashti, his servants sought beautiful young virgins to be brought to the king. Through a series of events, Esther, the cousin of Mordecai, found favor with the king and she was crowned as his queen instead of Vashti. However, the king did not know Esther was a Jew. Mordecai, who had raised Esther, also walked in the favor of the king because he had once given advice that had saved the king's life.

After this, Haman, an official in the court, was promoted by King Ahasuerus to sit above all the princes. This was a position of great honor and great authority. When the king's servants bowed to give him homage as the king had commanded, Mordecai would not bow or pay homage because he was a Jew, and this angered Haman. He was filled with wrath and fixed within his heart his determination to kill Mordecai and all the Jews.

Haman met with King Ahasuerus and told him of a people who would not obey the king's laws. He convinced the king to give him authority to annihilate all the Jews, both young and old, little children and women, on the 13th day of the 12th month (the month of Adar) and to plunder all their possessions. So a decree was written that the Jews were to be destroyed and letters were sent from the king by courier to every province.

Mordecai went to the city gate and got word to Esther that the decree had been issued and that she needed to go to the king and ask him for mercy for her people, the Jews. She sent word back to Mordecai to call for a fast with all Jews for her. She knew it was against the law for her to approach the king unannounced (Esther 4:16). Mordecai and all the Jews in the province of Shushan, as well as Esther and her maids, fasted for three days.

The result was a miracle from God. The Jews were victorious and the gallows that Haman made for Mordecai actually became the gallows on which Haman was hanged (Esther 7:10). The king revoked the letters devised by Haman to kill all the Jews, and instead permitted the Jews to protect their lives and destroy any people who would assault them.

There is an interesting conversation that takes place between Queen Esther and King Ahasuerus, starting in verse 12 of chapter 9 in the book of Esther:

> *And the king said to Queen Esther, "The Jews have killed and destroyed five hundred men in Shushan the citadel, and the ten sons of Haman. What have they done in the rest of the king's provinces? Now what is your petition? It shall be granted to you. Or what is your further request? It shall be done."*
>
> *Then Esther said, "If it pleases the king, let it be granted to the Jews who are in Shushan* **to do again tomorrow according to today's decree, and let Haman's ten sons be hanged on the gallows."**
>
> *So the king commanded this to be done; the decree was issued in Shushan, and they hanged Haman's ten sons.*
>
> ESTHER 9:12-14

Queen Esther's request seemed very strange to say the least. After all, the 10 sons of Haman had already been killed, so what would be the purpose in hanging them on the gallows?

In their writings, the rabbis and the *midrash* expound on the word *tomorrow*: "There is a tomorrow that is now and a tomorrow which is later" (Tanchuma Bo 13 and Rashi on Exodus 13:14). Another way of looking at this would be that Esther was prophesying that the hanging of Haman's 10 sons was not something that would be a stand-alone event but would be repeated in a future "tomorrow."

When we look at the book of Esther in the original Hebrew, there is something very unique. We see the listing of Haman's 10 sons (Esther 9:7-9) is written on a separate page in a very special way. On the right, the names of the 10 sons of Haman are listed in a column and written in extremely large letters. On the left is the word *v'et* (and), and this word is repeated 10 times in the left column.

According to the *Thirty-Two Rules of Eliezer*, when the word *v'et* is used, it signifies replication. This indicates that there was to be an additional hanging after the hanging of Haman's 10 sons. Also on this same page are three Hebrew letters that are written extremely small. They are the *taf*, the *shin*, and the *zayin*. The scribes always copy this page in this extreme manner.

The three small letters together form *taf-shin-zayin*, which could indicate the Jewish year 5707. On the Gregorian calendar, this corresponds to the year 1946. What happened in 1946?

In the year 1946, 23 Nazi war criminals were tried in the world-famous Nuremberg War Crimes Tribunal. Of these 23 Nazis, 11 were sentenced to be executed by hanging. But just two hours before the execution, one of the 11, Herman Goering, committed suicide so only 10 were hung.

Because this was a military tribunal, the normal methods of execution by firing squad or by the electric chair were set aside. The court specifically prescribed death by hanging for these 10 remaining men who had worked to eliminate the Jews.

Everything happened exactly as Queen Esther prophesied when she said her request for tomorrow was, "Let Haman's 10 sons be hanged." It's interesting to note that the 10 sons of Haman were descendants of Amalek, and many historians consider the 10 Nazis war criminals to also be descendants of Amalek.

Adolf Hitler knew that the Jews were connected to some supernatural and unseen power. This is obvious because of his fear of them. He even declared that anyone who was found to possess a copy of the book of Esther would immediately be executed.

Through the centuries, the Jews have celebrated the victory of Mordecai and Esther as a holiday called Purim. Because of this, many of the attacks by the Nazis on the Jewish people coincided with Purim (14 and 15 Adar).

In 1942, 10 Jews were hung in Zduńska Wola for the purpose of avenging the hanging of Haman's 10 sons. Likewise in 1943 the Nazis shot 10 Jews from the ghetto in Piotrków. That same year more than 100 Jewish doctors and their families were shot by the Nazis in Czestochowa on Purim. On January 30, 1944, Adolf Hitler made a speech where he said that if for any reason the Nazis were defeated, the Jews would celebrate "a second Purim."

The *New York Herald Tribune* of October 16, 1946, reported that Julius Streicher, one of the 10 to be hanged, "ascended to the gallows, and with burning hatred in his eyes, Streicher looked down at the witnesses and shouted his last words as he was hanged: 'Purim Fest 1946!'" The date of the execution (October 16, 1946) fell on the Jewish festival Hoshana Rabbah (21-Tishrei), which is known as the last days of judgment that begins on Rosh Hashana.

Although nearly 2,400 years had passed from the time Esther prophesied an additional hanging of 10, it eventually came to pass on the exact date as prophesied, as all true prophecies do.

The **Aleph** and the **Tav**

John 1:1 says, "In the beginning was the Word, and the Word was with God, and the Word was God." We know that in the Greek language there are two words for the word *word*. One is *logos* and the other is *rhema*. *Logos* is the written Word of God—the letters written on parchment. *Rhema* is the spoken, living, or revealed Word of God.

Many times in our Christian walk we read a scripture and possibly even memorize it. We feel we know it well. Then one day we hear this exact same scripture and it "comes alive" inside of us. The scripture that used to be *logos* became *rhema*. In other words, it was no longer just letters on a page, but the Word came alive and was revealed to us by the Holy Spirit.

It is interesting that in John chapter 1 it says, "In the beginning was the Word." And verse 14 tells us that the Word became flesh. In other words, the Word in verse 1 is clearly Jesus. You would think that the word *Word* in verse 1 would have come from the Greek word *rhema*, because Jesus is the living, spoken, revealed Word of God. But surprisingly, it is not. The Bible calls Jesus the written Word in John 1:1.

Several times in the New Testament Jesus calls Himself the "Alpha and the Omega," "the Beginning and the End," the "First and the Last" (Revelation 22:13). You can look up these scriptures in your English Bible and that is what it says. However, Jesus never said I am the Alpha and the Omega because He didn't speak Greek. He spoke Hebrew and Aramaic. What He actually said was, "I am the *Aleph* and the *Tav*."

The *Aleph* and the *Tav* are the first and last letters of the Hebrew alphabet. Because of that, the translators automatically assumed that Jesus was referring to the first and last letters of the Greek alphabet. In fact, there are Bible translations that say Jesus said He was the A and the Z. Jesus did not say He was the A and the Z, nor did He say He was the Alpha and the Omega, again because He did not speak English or Greek. He spoke Hebrew and Aramaic.

What He was referring to is this: In the first line of Genesis, the Book of Beginnings, in the first line of the Torah that every Jew knew well, were these words—*b'rasheet bara Elohim et HaShamayim v'et HaEretz. B'rasheet* is translated "in the beginning." *Bara* is translated "created." *Elohim* is rendered as "God." *HaShamayim* is translated "heavens." *V'et HaEretz* is translated "and the earth."

You may notice a word was skipped—the word *et.* The reason it was not translated is because the rabbis and scribes have never known the exact meaning of this word. The reason it was not eliminated from the text is because the Hebrew text is also a complicated mathematical formula, and nothing can be added or taken away. In the Hebrew language the word *et,* that has been untranslatable for thousands of years, is spelled *Aleph Tav.*

When Jesus said, "I am the *Aleph* and the *Tav,*" He was saying I am the Word, (the logos—written Word) that was in the beginning. In the first line of the Torah, in the first line of the first verse in Genesis, He was there with God. He was in the beginning and all things were created through Him.

So when John wrote the first line of his gospel, he wrote, "In the beginning was the Word" (Jesus, the Word of God) and the Word of God created everything. The Word came to earth and became the salvation of man.

> *In the beginning was the Word, and the Word was with God, and the Word was God. He was in the beginning with God. All things were made through Him, and without Him nothing was made that was made.*
>
> JOHN 1:1-3

It is evident that Jesus was not just referring to Himself as letters in the alphabet, but He specifically was saying that He was the Word of God who was in the beginning with God.

> **In the beginning** *God created the heavens and the earth.*
>
> Genesis 1:1

> **In the beginning** *was the Word* [logos]. *and the Word was with God, and the Word was God.*
>
> John 1:1

In the beginning was the Word and the Word was God. He created everything and set forth a plan for mankind to spend eternity with Him. In the end of time, the Lord will say, "It is done," and everything will have been completed that God set forth to do. His creation will be redeemed, forever partaking of the life He freely gives.

> *And He said to me, "It is done! I am the Alpha and the Omega, the Beginning and the End. I will give of the fountain of the water of life freely to him who thirsts."*
>
> Revelation 21:6

Epilogue

There is a cosmic war that has been raging from the beginning of time. This war is between good and evil, but deeper than that, the war is actually between the Creator and His creation that rebelled.

Satan has used all his resources to disrupt the ultimate plan of God. In every case he has failed, and he always will. The methods of medieval times don't work in this modern technologically advanced era, so his methods will continually be upgraded. But like in the times of the past, the deceptions of the enemy will come to nothing. As prophesied, the judgment of the enemy will be complete, and he will be forever banished from heaven, earth, and God's creation.

The Creator will never stop creating and there will always be manifestations of the supernatural beyond our ability to comprehend. Throughout eternity we will continue to marvel as we see manifestations of new things in unknown dimensions without end.

As a Christian, your best days are yet to come!

BIBLIOGRAPHY

CERN: https://home.cern/about/who-we-are/our-mission; accessed March 21, 2024.

Gardner, Martin. "Flat and Hollow," *Fads and Fallacies in the Name of Science,* 2nd ed. Mineola, NY: Dover Publications, 1957.

Hubble, Edwin. Astronomer, NASA.gov; https://science.nasa .gov/people/edwin-hubble/; accessed March 18, 2024.

Johnson, Ken. *Ancient Book of Enoch.* CreateSpace, 2012.

Lindsay, Dennis G. *Giants, Fallen Angels and the Return of the Nephilim.* Shippensburg, PA: Destiny Image Publishers, 2018.

National Geographic, Volume LXXVIII. Washington, DC: National Geographic Society, August 1940.

The Words of Flavius Josephus, Book V: Chapter II: The Antiquities of the Jews 3.

ABOUT
LARRY OLLISON

Dr. Larry Ollison is founder and senior pastor of Walk on the Water Faith Church and founder of Larry Ollison Ministries. He earned a B.A. and M.A. in Theology and a Ph.D. and Th.D. from LCU. With nearly sixty years in the ministry, Dr. Ollison ministers the Word through all media means available. Dr. Ollison also has an extensive business background and has served as President of the Marine Dealers' Association, Chairman of the Missouri State Marine Board, and also served on the boards of several banks and corporations. He is a pilot.

His business background brings a unique flavor to his teaching. His focus areas are the blood of Jesus, faith, relationships, Hebrew language, the Holy Spirit, end times, heaven, and other topics that aren't typically taught from the pulpit. During ministry, he operates freely in the gifts of the Holy Spirit. His use of humor and ability to make theological concepts simple makes it enjoyable and easy for everyone to understand. Countless testimonies have been received from people who say their lives have been changed after experiencing Dr. Ollison's unique ministry.

Dr. Ollison's current media ministries include LarryOllisonRadio.com, author of *The Cutting Edge* daily devotional, weekly live-stream broadcasts, author for Harrison House Publishing, as well as many social media platforms.

He was the co-founder and Vice-President of Spirit FM Christian Radio Network for 39 years, which was comprised of 24 Christian music stations in Missouri, and heard worldwide through the online stream. The ministry now programs the online worship format, ElevateWorship.Online.

Dr. Ollison serves other ministries as well: Executive board member of Billye Brim Ministries, Vice-Chairman of Prophecy Watchers, Dean of 3BI (an accredited Bible college), and Missouri State Director for Christians United for Israel (CUFI). Dr. Ollison was one of the 400 original CUFI members and the organization now has over ten million members worldwide.

He is also an international speaker and has spoken at numerous conventions in Australia, New Zealand, and Europe and made many trips to Israel for research and classroom education. His number-one goal is to meet the needs of people through teaching faith in God's Word.

YOUR HOUSE OF
FAITH

Sign up for a **FREE** subscription to the
Harrison House digital magazine and get
excellent content delivered directly to your inbox!
harrisonhouse.com/signup

Sign up for Messages that Equip You to Walk in the Abundant Life

• Receive biblically sound and Spirit-filled
encouragement to focus on and maintain your faith
• Grow in faith through biblical teachings, prayers, and
other spiritual insights
• Connect with a community of believers who share your
values and beliefs

)erience Fresh Teachings and piration to Build Your Faith

pen your understanding of God's purpose for
ife
connected and inspired on your faith journey
rn how to grow spiritually in your walk with God

In the Right Hands, This Book Will Change Lives!

Most of the people who need this message will not be looking for this book. To change their lives, you need to **put a copy of this book in their hands.**

Our ministry is constantly seeking methods to find the people who need this anointed message to change their lives. **Will you help us reach these people?**

Extend this ministry by sowing three, five, ten, or *even more* books today and change people's lives for the better! Your generosity will be part of catalyzing the Great Awakening that many have been prophesying and praying for.

From

Dr. Larry Ollison

Unimaginable Beauty Awaits in Your Future Home

What Christian isn't curious about heaven? Although heaven is discussed extensively in the Bible, centuries of fictional characterizations of the afterlife have left most believers with an inaccurate picture of what heaven is really like.

In *A Place Called Heaven,* author, pastor, and scholar Dr. Larry Ollison searches the entire Bible for rock-solid answers to your deepest questions about heaven.

Dr. Ollison tackles questions like...

- What happens when you die?
- What is the Paradise of God?
- Where is heaven, and what does it look like?
- How will our heavenly bodies be different?
- Are loved ones there waiting for us and will they recognize us?

Each chapter illustrates a biblically accurate and magnificent picture of heaven. As your excitement and anticipation for your future home builds, you'll be convinced beyond any doubt that a glorious future awaits you in *A Place Called Heaven!*

Purchase your copy wherever books are sold

From

Dr. Larry Ollison

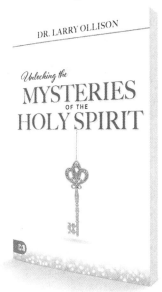

Mystery Solved! You've Been Given Power for Life

The Holy Spirit may seem like a mystery to many Christians and an abstract religious idea to others. But if you're born again, He's the very Spirit of God living inside of you and supernaturally connecting you to heaven!

Dr. Larry Ollison, a popular speaker nationally and internationally for more than 40 years, explains this third person of the Trinity is not spooky, weird, or an actual ghost. He's not even a something—but a Someone you can know personally and intimately.

In *Unlocking the Mysteries of the Holy Spirit,* Dr. Larry shares simply and scripturally that the Holy Spirit is your life-long guide to victory. He never leaves you alone, He equips you with wisdom, grace, and power to face any circumstance, and He knows more about your future than you know about your past.

Dr. Ollison outlines...

- The personality of the Holy Spirit – His likes and dislikes
- His assignment on the earth today
- How the gifts of the Spirit operate and how we cooperate

You will become more spiritually in tune page by page as you get better acquainted with the power of the Holy Spirit that Jesus said *you need* for life!

Purchase your copy wherever books are sold